Keats and the Sublime

Leads him perplex'd, where he may likeliest find 525
Truce to his restless thoughts, and entertain
The irksome hours, till his great chief return.
Part on the plain, or in the air sublime,
Upon the wing, or in swift race contend,
As at the Olympian games or Pythian fields ;   530
Part curb their fiery steeds, or shun the goal
With rapid wheels, or fronted brigades form.
As when, to warn proud cities, war appears
Waged in the troubled sky, and armies rush
To battle in the clouds, before each van   535
Prick forth the airy knights, and couch their spears
Till thickest legions close ; with feats of arms
From either end of Heaven the welkin burns.
Others, with vast Typhœan rage more fell,
Rend up both rocks and hills, and ride the air 540
In whirlwind ; Hell scarce holds the wild uproar.
As when Alcides, from Œchalia crown'd
With conquest, felt the envenom'd robe, and tore
Through pain up by the roots Thessalian pines,
And Lichas from the top of Œta threw   545
Into the Euboic sea.   Others more mild,
Retreated in a silent valley, sing
With notes angelical to many a harp
Their own heroic deeds and hapless fall
By doom of battle ; and complain that fate   550
Free virtue should inthrall to force or chance.
Their song was partial, but the harmony
(What could it less when Spirits immortal sing ?)
Suspended Hell, and took with ravishment   554
The thronging audience.   In discourse more sweet
(For eloquence the soul, song charms the sense,)
Others apart sat on a hill retired,
In thoughts more elevate, and reason'd high
Of providence, foreknowledge, will, and fate,
Fix'd fate, free will, foreknowledge absolute, 560

A leaf from Keats's copy of *Paradise Lost*, with his marginal annotations. Reproduced by permission of the London Borough of Camden from the collections at Keats House, Hampstead.

Keats and the Sublime

Stuart A. Ende

New Haven and London   Yale University Press

1976

Published with assistance from the
Kingsley Trust Association Publication Fund
established by the Scroll and Key Society of Yale College.

Library of Congress catalog card number: 76-8420
International standard book number: 0-300-02010-4

Designed by John O. C. McCrillis
and set in Baskerville type.
Printed in the United States of America by
The Vail-Ballou Press, Inc., Binghamton, N.Y.

Published in Great Britain, Europe, Africa, and Asia
(except Japan) by Yale University Press, Ltd.,
London. Distributed in Latin America by Kaiman
& Polon, Inc., New York City; in Australia and
New Zealand by Book & Film Services, Artarmon, N.S.W.,
Australia; in Japan by John Weatherhill, Inc., Tokyo.

Acknowledgment is made to the Macmillan Publishing Co.,
Inc., New York, and to M. B. Yeats, Miss Anne Yeats, and
the Macmillan Co. of London and Basingstoke for permission to quote from the following works by W. B. Yeats: *Essays and Introductions,* © Mrs. W. B. Yeats 1961; *A Vision,* copyright 1937 by William Butler Yeats, renewed 1965 by Bertha Georgie Yeats and Anne Butler Yeats; *Collected Poems:* "Ego Dominus Tuus," copyright 1918 by Macmillan Publishing Co., Inc., renewed 1946 by Bertha Georgie Yeats; "A Dialogue of Self and Soul," "Blood and the Moon," "Crazy Jane Talks with the Bishop," copyright 1933 by Macmillan Publishing Co., Inc., renewed 1961 by Bertha Georgie Yeats; "The Wild Old Wicked Man," "The Man and the Echo," copyright 1940 by Georgie Yeats, renewed 1968 by Bertha Georgie Yeats, Michael Butler Yeats, and Anne Yeats.

For Susan

whose smile . . .

The description of the employments of the [fallen] angels . . . is the most perfect example of mingled pathos and sublimity.

Hazlitt, "On Shakspeare and Milton"

Milton is godlike in the sublime pathetic.

Keats, annotation to *Paradise Lost*

Contents

Preface

Keats thought that if poetry did not come as naturally and inevitably as leaves to a tree, it had better not come at all. If poetry be seen as a response to a text, where the text is some form of reality read as a text, then criticism, which also involves relationship to text, also should appear to come inevitably. Yeats, for example, claimed that if we knew the first principle of any religion—religion being a full form of exegesis—we would know how it would end, were it given time in which to do so. Criticism does not always have this fullness, but there are moments during which the critic, as ideal reader and commentator, seems to stand at the center of the text and, surrendering himself to the cosmos that is the work around him, reports the coherence of that cosmos almost as a reflexive response—given his location and his yielding, his pronouncements seem inevitable. He seeks to impose no categories, to name no names, for to do so would be to exert his power over the text, to capture its spherical quality on the flat planes of his intellectual reach.

Yet if he does not name and order, the commentator risks the danger of losing his vision (and report) to the text, of being possessed by it rather than possessing it—he becomes merely a viewer or reader. We approach texts for relief, or delight, or perhaps as Yeats says, for the forgiveness of sin, and so we tend to idealize them, at least at first, and grant them a certain power. This is a power over us, as well as over the "reality" they comprehend, and the reader who would describe his vision necessarily puts off that power and clears a space within which to find his own voice. Such an effort at control need not be willful, but it does seem necessary, for without a mild exercise of power, the text retains its ambivalent aspect of otherness; control, on the other hand, leads to possession.

These two opposed movements, which we usefully may

xi

think of as intellectual and emotional in their respective extremes of yielding and retaining self-possession, seem always operative in textual encounters, and their ratio is one description of a reader's approach. We can formulate an ideal approach, which would consist in striking a balance, in which the reader does not cease to need or love the text yet retains some of his power to define, to see properly, and to report. Whatever name we choose for this relationship will necessarily be paradoxical or oxymoronic, for it will need to comprehend outer and inner, expansion and contraction, contact and withdrawal.

The poet seems to operate with a similar dynamic, though his strategies may be less obvious. His "text" must be similarly (or more greatly) idealized, yet he must not surrender self or identity to it. A critic who surrenders self becomes merely a reader, but a poet who surrenders to what appears to be outside himself loses his poetic voice. "Reading" of this committed sort thus requires a submission that is, finally, an act of love, and a statement of homage perhaps, and it seems necessary for poets; yet it cannot be a finality, or we may have no poems. Yeats, whom I take as one of our most revealing commentators on poetic creativity, claims that the *ideal* response consists in being "self-possessed in self-surrender," a paradox that embraces the simultaneous gain and loss experienced by the poet in his encounter with the romance of texts.

Poets—perhaps like other men and women—do not begin with this consciousness of dualism. Rather, they grow into it, and one of the subthemes of the present study is the changing relation of the poet to the otherness that is text, which is a way of viewing poetic development. Suppose we consider Milton's Satan, recently fallen into an awareness of his own dualism, as a mature, subjective poet. Others have suggested the conceit of Satan as poet; but let us briefly view him in the act of reading a "text"—his first sight of Adam and Eve in the garden. This is a "text" he has seen before, in the remembrances of the mind's eye, for the innocent pair recalls Satan to his earlier self. Yet they are new to him as well, and these elements together create an ambivalence in Satan that makes him recoil initially from their unexpected beauty. As he continues to stare, however, he softens and allows their "Divine resemblance" to make a claim upon his love: "O Hell!" he begins, with an infernal pun,

> what do mine eyes with grief behold,
> Into our room of bliss thus high advanc'd
> Creatures of other mould, earth-born perhaps,
> Not Spirits, yet to heav'nly Spirits bright
> Little inferior; whom my thoughts pursue
> With wonder, and could love.
>
> [*Paradise Lost,* IV, 358–63]

"And could love": the relationship of fallen reader to innocent text focuses on this emotional pivot. Satan could love Adam and Eve for their proximity to Spirits that are yet unfallen, as he was, not so long ago: if he were to love them, one component of his love would consist in loving himself in them. But to do so is to give up his own selfhood as identity, which feels "grief" at the sight of them because that identity is a consequence of Satan's own fall. So at the last moment, before "could" becomes "do," he draws back, pleading the necessity of his own selfhood, his own "Empire":

> And should I at your harmless innocence
> Melt, as I do, yet public reason just,
> Honor and Empire with revenge enlarg'd,
> By conquering this new World, compels me now
> To do what else though damn'd I should abhor.
>
> [IV, 388–92]

Were Satan to continue to "melt," as indeed he begins to do, he would lose the possibility of enlarging that selfhood, which results, alas, only from conquering those of Adam and Eve. He can love only to a point, for a complete love of otherness means loss of self-possession.

One does not want to insist on the validity of every element of the analogy between Satan and poet or reader: Coleridge reminds us that few similes walk on all fours. Yet the general dynamic seems accurate. One question that the analogy does not answer fully is, what is it that takes the place of Adam and Eve for the poet? What "text" evokes the contrary feelings of love and a desire for self-retention? A quick, general answer would be, everything the poet has idealized. Keats wrote Reynolds that "I have not the slightest feel of humility towards the Public—or to any thing in existence,—but the eternal Being, the Principle of Beauty,—and the Memory of great Men." The poet was feeling somewhat put upon when he wrote that letter—Reynolds, among other friends, had not cared for Keats's original preface to *Endymion*—but his statement of the things that do genuinely evoke his humility will do as an example of idealization. The "eternal Being," beauty, one's idea of the great men who have gone before—these sometimes indistinguishable ideals constitute, in Keats and in Yeats among other poets we will consider, poetic sublimity, the state of being to which poetic ecstasy may transport him. What holds him back, as it were, is a form of self-regard that is not merely the selfhood, as in Satan, but his love for natural things, his wish for a sensual happiness, even one taken up into the mind.

This, briefly stated, is the conflict the following chapters trace, as a poet such as Keats portrays encounters which evoke incompatible desires: to be sublimed in the ecstasy that is poetic fire, and to retain one's sentient being. This simple incompatibility is complicated both by a poet's development, which changes his relation to both spheres of existence, and by an ambivalence that exists from the start in a poet's feelings toward an idealized or sublime otherness. I have invoked the difficult, sometimes cumbersome, but nevertheless illuminating theories of Freud in treating these complications and have tried for the most part to correlate these theories with the critical statements of Yeats, whom I take as one of our most significant writers on the Romantic experience. Yeats needs no justification in a study of this type, but Freud may, especially since, as I think, he has been badly used quite often before. I do not think lyrical poetry divulges as much of its motivation to the theories of either dream or sexuality as it does to Freud's overall theory of the relation of subject to object, man to the outer world, and the subjective drama wherein this relation is played. This differs radically from the "psychoanalytic" approach we usually meet in literary criticism, but it is justified, I believe, by a sustained reading of the whole of Freud's work. It is, in fact, what Freud is "about," the central situation of his work on the relations of the ego. And it is in this form that Freud has proved attractive to such readers as Thomas Mann and Kenneth Burke. I discuss Burke in the text, but here is Mann, on the occasion of Freud's eightieth birthday:

> . . . unless I am greatly mistaken, it is just this confrontation of object and subject, their mingling and identification, the resultant insight into the mysterious unity of ego and actuality, destiny and character, doing and happening, and thus into the mystery of reality as an operation of the psyche—it is just this confrontation that is the alpha and omega of all psychoanalytical knowledge. [*Freud and the Future*]

If we emphasize the subjectivity of the experience of relation, we have a remarkably discerning view of Freud.

Keats as poet is everywhere concerned with encounters, and I derive from Freud's work on the ego's relation to outer reality and to the unconscious, and from various of Yeats's prose statements, a complicated picture of poetic encounters. It might be well to set out the outlines of the picture here. The starting point, for both men, is a form of unity that Yeats calls wholeness and Freud, narcissism. This is broken, inevitably, by the world breaking faith, in Yeats's view, and by object-loss, in Freud's. We are now at the true beginning of subjective poetry, Yeats believes, for the subjective poet seeks to regain a wholeness he knows is lost, in an effort to achieve Unity of Being. That Unity is both internal and external—it yokes together the paired terms that Mann provides—though the path to it is manifoldly difficult, since reality, in Mann's words, is now an operation of the psyche. Accordingly, the subjective poet must deal with two distinct and conflicting demands placed upon him: one, for a return of the lost relationship and the instinctual or natural happiness it provided; and another, the satisfaction of the idealized other, the daemon of sublimity, a portion of mind that seems to grow harsher and more powerful following loss. Yeats interprets this as a conflict between primary and antithetical desires. The elements of Freud that are most helpful in this context are his notions of internalization, by which what had been lost is recreated in the mind, and the ego's relation to the ego ideal, the harsh voice that, as I shall suggest, functions much like Yeats's daemon.

I think it is the distinction between these that determines the beneficent or daemonic aspect of the muse that Keats, like the Miltonic poets of the eighteenth century, invokes in her various forms. The beneficent or "softer" muse usually makes possible the restoration of an earlier situation; the antithetical or daemonic muse, the muse of terror, places further demands upon the poet. Though both forms exist in each of the poets I consider, and though one can hardly evaluate each with regard to the other, there is a discernible difference in voice and in the psychopoetic situation in each case. By a process akin to Freudian identification, the beneficent muse—Joseph Warton's Fancy, or Keats's Psyche—gives promise of a joining or union that provides the poet with the opportunity of a repetition of an earlier pleasure: she thus is associated with poetic bliss, a favorite term in post-Miltonic poetry. The alternative, which is a penseroso mode (as beneficence derives from *L'Allegro*), finds the poet confronting an otherness that is antithetical to his desires, even though he had earlier idealized this other as a form of the sublime. The relationship here becomes a dialogue of reconciliation, in which the poet must "read" properly, must go beyond Satan's hesitating love, and so enter relationship with a greatness that threatens his being. It is during the course of such a dialogue, however brief or implicit, that poetic voice achieves a remarkably lyrical intensity, as the poet both chastens his own desire and humanizes a voice of terror by justifying his own emotional self and his wish to retain the idea of sublimity. Poetic strength here is the capacity for paradox and mingled contraries, the necessary gain and loss of relation: not Hazlitt's partial separation of sublimity and pathos voiced in the epigraph to this book, but Keats's acceptance of inevitable oxymoron—the "sublime pathetic."

Terminology is a problem for a study of this kind. There are, first, the difficulties with literary terms. "Sublime" has a long history of imprecise meanings (though everyone always seemed to know what was meant) and, even before Keats wrote, was a subject for burlesque: "Come—one bottle more—and have at the sublime," Burns scoffs in *The Whistle*. Moreover, "sublimation" as a psychological term has much more to do with the opposite of the "sublime" than the homonymous similarity would lead us to expect, or hope. And in general, Freud's terms seem ponderous and reductive next to those of the poets. This I think is unfortunate (though a logical consequence of his effort to seem scientific), for Freud usually treats compelling states of existence with subtlety and acute sensitivity—though one yet may be irked by the impersonality of the terms of that most personal inquiry. One hopes, at last, that the contexts will define the terms, that the scheme of poet and other will provide a suitable context, and that the approach justifies the inevitable difficulties of language and conceptualization.

ACKNOWLEDGMENTS

For their gracious help I wish to thank Christina M. Gee and Margaret Van Reenan, curators of the Keats House in Hampstead. The administrators of the Graves Awards at Pomona College and the Division of the Humanities and Social Sciences at Caltech made it possible for me to visit Hampstead and gave me time in which to write. Joanne Clark typed the manuscript with much good humor and too few dinners. *ELH: A Journal of English Literary History* has granted permission to reprint with modification sections of my article, "Keats's Music of Truth," which appeared in the Spring 1973 issue.

Finally, acknowledgments seem to me to imply often debts that cannot be repaid, since Milton's "perfect Diapason" depends upon a finer response than this writer at least can make. Those gifted critics who have pointed to the depths of Romantic poetry will recognize my indebtedness; as will another gifted critic, my wife, Susan Ende, who has mused these pages with me.

1

Milton and the Subjective Drama of the Eighteenth-Century Sublime Poem

> The fame of the great names we look up to is immortal:
> and shall not we who contemplate it imbibe a portion of
> ethereal fire, the *divinae particula aurae,* which nothing
> can extinguish?
>
> Hazlitt, *On the Feeling of Immortality in Youth*

Part of the great legacy that Milton left for those poets who, like Collins, necessarily sought to follow his "guiding steps," consists of clear illustrations of the poet's ability to convert loss in the world to subjective gain. Though the outer landscape might have faded with his eyesight, Milton proclaims that he "not the more" ceases "to wander where the Muses haunt," for their locus is at least in part the mind and "all her powers." With difficulty but with no uncertainty, Milton depicted his power to revisit that compensatory locus, the main region of the invocations in *Paradise Lost.* Partly because of just this certainty, however, it proved difficult to be one of the great poet's legatees: nor does it seem as if Thomson, Collins, Gray, Akenside, the Wartons, and numerous others who sought the happy fields of subjective compensation could help but choose Milton as their poetic model. The consequence of this choice is the disturbingly harmonious note of frustrated poetic desire sounded in much of the better post-Miltonic poetry of the mid-eighteenth century and after, as if a powerful example of poetic riches necessitated an ensuing sense of exclusion from inner strength.

This sense of exclusion is frequently followed, as if by reflex, by an attempted restoration, in which the poet seeks a union with a muse or power that comprehends both a personified outerness and an aspect of mind. Where the emphasis falls here may well depend upon a reader's approach. Geoffrey Hartman, with a view toward literary history, sees the power as a form of the genius loci: eighteenth-century poetry of the sublime, he writes, "projects a sacred marriage," in which the invocation of "the ghost in the landscape is only preparatory to a deeper ceremonial merging of the poet's spirit and spirit of place. . . ." [1] It is also possible to consider the dynamics of the confrontation in more subjective terms—the "merging" in this case is with a projected aspect of self as much as with a spirit of place. Yeats emphasizes the importance of this view in his insistence that, regardless of the apparent subject of a poem, a poet writes always of his "personal life." [2] In any case, that encounters of this type are widespread in both pre-Romantic and Romantic lyric poems hardly needs reiteration to readers, though Victor Brombert's identification of the "central metaphor" of Rousseau's subjectivity introduces an interesting Continental parallel: " 'ce séjour isolé oú je m'étais enlacé de moi-même . . .' ('where I did entwine with myself')." [3] Though I shall suggest that in the poetry such entwining evades solipsism, it nevertheless informs the "epiphany" Hartman is led to discuss: "what modern literary theory tends to call an epiphany involves a confrontation with a second self in the form of genius loci or Persona." [4]

As an internal joining, the dynamic shares important characteristics with certain psychical interrelations that Freud describes and that may illuminate the poet's relation to otherness. Though it is now thirty-five years since his death, it is still not easy to introduce Freud's thought to a literary discussion, partly because of the narrow translation of his ideas made by some early "Freudian" critics, and partly because even now most commentators invoke Freud as an explicator of symbols, the creator of the sexual lexicon of a subtler language. But this is to reduce the greater part of Freud's work, and to overlook the Freud of *On Narcissism, The Ego and the Id,* and the various "metapsychological" papers, all of which concern themselves most importantly with the relation of subject to object, self to other.

It is also remarkable that about thirty-five years have passed since Kenneth Burke, one of our most far-reaching and humane critics, wrote his seminal essay *Freud—and the Analysis of Poetry*. Burke's achievement in the essay is two-fold: he defines the essential character of Freud's thought, and he suggests its use for the analysis of poetry. There is an assumption that underlies Burke's approach and helps to formulate what we might term his own strategy: Burke finds Freud to be not the great indicter of human existence but one of its heroes, for "over the great course of his work, it is the matter of human rescue that he is concerned with," and "the very essence of his studies, even at their most forbidding moments (in fact, precisely at those moments), is charitableness, a concern with salvation." [5]

With this epitome of Freud's concern, Burke proceeds to the "area of overlap" between psychoanalytic formulations and aesthetic theory, which he finds in this insight of Freud's: "The acts of the neurotic are symbolic acts." Lionel Trilling, also at about this time, composed his essay *Art and Neurosis* to "rescue" the artist precisely from the charge of being neurotic.[6] Burke, more deftly and resourcefully, avoids the quarrel with Freud in favor of an approach that takes full advantage of congruence while recognizing dissimilarity.

> The acts of the neurotic are symbolic acts. Hence in so far as both the neurotic act and the poetic act share this property in common, they may share a terminological chart in common. But in so far as they deviate, terminology likewise must deviate. And this deviation is a fact that literary criticism must explicitly consider.[7]

Burke wishes to broaden Freud by extending the "psychological" approach to a poem to include "sociological" values ("the total act of human communication") and to change Freud's implied emphasis on expressionism to more rhetorical grounds, in which we take account of the relation of poem to reader as well as poet to poem. He argues that "whereas the expressionistic emphasis reveals the way in which the poet with an attitude embodies it in appropriate gesture, communication deals with the choice of gesture for the inducement of corresponding attitudes." [8] This perspective makes him somewhat unhappy with Freud's notion that art is founded on desire: Burke prefers to view the work of art as part of the category of "communication" rather than wish. Nevertheless, the separation between the categories is not clear. In developing his argument, Burke suggests that the "communicative function" of poetry is to invite the reader to "make himself over in the image of the imagery." Yet perhaps this says more about the motive for reading than writing, and in annotating the essay for republication, Burke notes that "I have since come to realize that 'communication' is itself but a technical species of 'love,' hence always lurks about the edges of the Freudian 'Libido.' " [9]

We ought to assume, with Burke, that the reader participates in the poet's "communication," but it is problematic whether the poet "communicates" with the reader or only with otherness. And in fact Burke's essay seems to support the latter more strongly than the former, for Burke (who seems incapable of missing the heart of a matter) finds poetry to consist in a "symbolic act" that comprises the poet's own "ritual drama." The "drama" is the "eventfulness" of a poem and is a consequence of the way in which a poet chooses and defines his words. "He finds some experience or relationship typical, or recurrent, or significant enough for him to need a word for it." But the word does not merely name the object, it "names vindictively, or plaintively, or promisingly, or consolingly, etc." And in this sense, all namings "are enactments, with every form of expression being capable of treatment as the efficient extension of one aspect or another of ritual drama." This is a "drama" that comprehends both inner and outer, then, and is further glossed by this parenthetic note: "even the scientific essay would have its measure of choreography, its pedestrian pace itself being analyzed as gesture or incantation, its polysyllables being as style the mimetics of a distinct monasticism, etc." [10] The inner plot of a poetic "drama" is characteristically one of redemption, in Burke's view, a rhetorical strategy whereby the poet dramatizes a symbolic effort to achieve a form of salvation, however momentary or fragile. Rhetoric has a psychological dimension; the psyche seeks intimations of its own power.

Burke concludes by supposing that a proper extension of Freud into the "major events" of a poem might take the form of "the analysis of role: salvation . . . typical relationships . . . modes of acceptance, rejection, self-acceptance," and so on. This bristling idea of the poem as a ritual drama that presents the poet (or speaker) in a role in which he attempts to achieve salvation throws an added light on Yeats's "First Principle" of poetry, that "A poet writes always on his personal life. . . ." By "personal life" Yeats intends "emotional life," and if we view his principle in the context Burke provides, we may have a preliminary analytic framework in which to place extensions of Freud: the plot of the subjective poem is a personal drama, an allegory of emotional existence that seeks in otherness signs of wholeness; and the manner of this seeking may assume a form that is illuminated by a consideration of psychological processes.

Freud himself thought that typical emotional development followed a path from a primary stage of self-love to a point at which the individual reaches out to the world for his loved objects and so enters a state of relationship. The stage of self-love or "narcissism" is characterized by the id choosing the ego as its desired object. This self-involvement perhaps is necessary biologically, but Freud thought that the capacity for external relations represents a higher level of existence. Moreover, he recognized, and this is perhaps the most significant idea in *On Narcissism: An Introduction,* that once an outer relationship has been established, a loss of the object—which may be a person, a landscape, even an abstract idea—might *reverse* the usual course of development, resulting in a renewed or "secondary" narcissism. "The libido that has been withdrawn from the external world," as Freud explains the process, "has been directed to the ego once more." [11]

Freud looked with mistrust upon the renewal of narcis-

sism and no doubt would have viewed with misgivings such
self-satisfactions as Rousseau's self-entwining. Yet Yeats, far
more a believer in the gifts of imagination, declared that the
subjective poet is born as poet at the moment he recognizes
that his fate is to experience outer loss: "a hero loves the
world till it breaks him," Yeats writes, "and the poet till it has
broken faith. . . ." So it is that the subjective poet finds his
nativity "in disappointment"; [12] from this point on he turns
to the compensatory imaginings of otherness. Where Freud
sees a desire for self-love, Yeats sees an attempt to restore a
state of wholeness. Both would agree, I think, that the poet
seeks a form of self-completion, however different might be
their evaluations of the attempt. If for the moment we put
aside this difference, we can consider that Yeats's wholeness
may be necessary for the creation of the Romantic (and pre-
Romantic) lyric: Hartman believes that "the Romantic 'I'
emerges nostalgically when certainty and simplicity of self
are lost. In a lyric poem it is clearly not the first-person form
that moves us (the poem need not be in the first person) but
rather the I toward which that I reaches. The very confusion
in modern literary theory concerning the fictive I . . . may
reflect a dialectic inherent in poetry between the relatively
self-conscious self and that self within the self which resem-
bles Blake's 'emanation' and Shelley's 'epipsyche.' " [13]

The problem for us as readers is that both Freud's and
Yeats's models appear to be incomplete, for the tendency to
self-completion in the poems takes two forms, not one, and
these are radically different. Poets of the pre-Romantic sublime tend not to pass into the frame and engage that sublime
otherness directly; but when they do attempt to go beyond
the moving withdrawals of Gray, let us say, they frequently
encounter a power that either threatens or consoles but does
not heal division. With great comprehensiveness, Norman
Maclean has traced these two aspects of the power to Aris-
totle's categories of fear and pity. [14] From the point of view
of the "I" that does the encountering, the power either stubbornly maintains the poet's exclusion or tentatively offers
the satisfaction of a form of sensual bliss that is compensa-

tory but contrary to the higher imagination. Let us glance at this case in which the muse appears to be beneficent rather than daemonic. Joseph Warton, who is as indebted to Milton as William Collins is, but who is not as self-conscious about the debt, invokes what at first seems imaginative power in his ode *To Fancy:*

> Then lay me by the haunted stream
> Wrapt in some wild, poetic dream
> In converse while methinks I rove
> With Spenser thro' a fairy grove;
> Till, suddenly awake, I hear
> Strange whisper'd music in my ear,
> And my glad soul in bliss is drown'd.
>
> [ll. 41–47]

James Thomson similarly had asked that Nature "lay me by the lowly brook / And whisper to my dreams" (*Autumn,* ll. 1371–72). For both poets the source is Milton's *L'Allegro,* which invites

> Such sights as youthful Poets dream
> On Summer eves by haunted stream.
>
> [ll. 129–30]

But Warton desires the "dream" only as a means of attaining the "bliss" of suffusion, the "soul" drowned in "whisper'd music." To drown in this manner paradoxically is to live again in the self-compensating solitude of subjective completion, as the ode goes on to suggest:

> The pangs of absence, O remove,
> For thou canst place me near my love,
> Canst fold in visionary bliss,
> And let me think I steal a kiss,
> While her ruby lips dispense
> Luscious nectar's quintessence!
>
> [ll. 73–78]

The "pangs of absence" Warton mentions may be real enough, but they seem to imply a subtle form of self-betrayal

rather than loss of something external, for the "love" he is
reunited with is a dimension of subjectivity, a gift of the self
to the self. Absence necessarily implies distance; yet the
"folding" here has much less to do with an actual "love" than
with the internal relationships of mind. Like Rousseau's
"entwining" and Yeats's knittedness of man to daemon, Warton's blissful folding suggests a reunion of ego and unconscious, and perhaps a removal of the internal danger that
developed when the self began to love and so became dependent upon outer things. Fancy, who makes all this possible, emerges as a self-compensating power of mind, the au-
tonomous and self-sufficient quality that enables mind to
exist apart from outward circumstance (the true "absence"),
and even to defy it. Warton's "visionary bliss" is only projected, he does not achieve it in the poem, yet his hope for it
represents one expression of the poet's faith in the beneficence of otherness.

The turn from Warton to Collins is the turn from imaginative bliss to a purified imagination, or from *L'Allegro* to the
higher strains of *Il Penseroso*. Milton's "companion" poems
confer upon the eighteenth century a distinction that is crucial to the poetry of the sublime, which, in this view, is actually the poetry of two distinct modes, only one of which
comprehends poetic sublimation—the realization of the wish
for poetic ecstasy. As alternative representations, both *L'Allegro* and *Il Penseroso* begin with statements of exclusion,
where what is being excluded in each is the other. Rosemund Tuve would demur from this, suggesting instead that
"Each poem begins with a banishing of the *travesty* of what is
praised in the other," [15] but it is a measure of the strength of
the renunciation of each speaker that the alternative is tra-
vestied: if only a travesty were rejected, how compelling
would the choice be?

"The act of choice is the essential creative act for Milton,"
Leslie Brisman observes in a very important recent study of
the poet.[16] The companion poems proffer two alternatives
and represent two forms of self-denial, or two selves being
denied. Each poem begins with "Hence," as Brisman notes, a

dismissal of the particular world that opposes the vision of the poem. The ultimate antagonist of the freedom of the mind in each poem is the realm of "eating cares" (*L'Allegro,* l. 135) that we associate with external reality. But once the speaker chooses mind over this, two separate modes become available.

The speaker in *L'Allegro* chooses the substitutive satisfaction of "heart-easing Mirth," a form of what Yeats would call "emotional" compensation, which is concerned always with restoring a lost satisfaction. Antithetical poets such as Yeats are mistrustful of such choices, for they seem to reiterate (though in the finer tone of the mind) the satisfactions given up in the natural world. The goal of "emotional" completion is always renewal or return, the repossession of the sources of the heart's ease, which do not change. It would be mistaken to see *L'Allegro's* odyssey as only a search for a sublimated physical satisfaction, for the broad goal he seeks is a form of freedom: "And in thy right hand lead with thee / The mountain nymph, sweet Liberty" (ll. 35–36). Yet his freedom is the freedom of pastoral, which in the poem takes the form of "unreprovèd pleasures free" (l. 40)., the sensual happiness of natural plenitude. Yeats thought that the happiness of nature was always, finally, a form of the happiness of the body; and that poets who seek it have, like William Morris, "but one story to tell us, how some man or woman lost and found again the happiness that is always half of the body." The "again" here is fundamental to natural happiness, which Yeats believes forms "links that chain the days to one another." In love with the succession of days, those who choose this form of happiness "do not seek in love that ecstasy, which Shelley's nightingale called death, that extremity of life in which life seems to pass away like the Phoenix in a flame of its own lighting, but rather a gentle self-surrender that would lose more than half its sweetness if it lost the savour of coming days." [17]

To chain the days, to hope that one moment follows another and so makes "again" possible, suggests a successiveness that perhaps explains the additive quality of the pleasures in *L'Allegro,* which Brisman interprets as an "and" poem, as opposed to the frequent "or" of *Il Penseroso.* "And" is a kin of "again," we recognize, whereas "or" suggests the successive lost natural possibilities the self will allow on its journey to the "ecstasy" Yeats sees as the opposite goal to that of natural poetry. Ecstasy, the world slipping away, implies a power—such as that which makes "Hell grant what Love did seek" in *Il Penseroso*—but natural succession is imbued with the idea of return:

> That Orpheus' self may heave his head
> From golden slumber on a bed
> Of heaped Elysian flowers, and hear
> Such strains as would have won the ear
> Of Pluto, to have quite set free
> His half-regained Eurydice.
>
> [ll. 145–50]

Eurydice's projected freedom I think epitomizes the freedom sought throughout the poem by the speaker. Her freedom would make possible further repetitions, the seeming beneficence of continuity. Such moments joined each to each may ease the heart, as only the emotional "savour of coming days" can. But in the two worlds of the companion poems, neither sphere of existence is complete, since each at least lacks the other. The speaker in *Il Penseroso* seeks not continuity but a discontinuity that is necessary to the kind of ecstasy Yeats associates with Shelley, and which we meet at the conclusion of Milton's poem. There is a suggestion in the poem of the isolation that attends such a choice, since the flame of one's own lighting distances the self from the company of men devoted to natural plenitude: "Oft on a plat of rising ground / I hear the far-off curfew sound / Over some wide-watered shore" (ll. 73–75). Nevertheless, Penseroso's burden is less this separation that results from his own "rising" toward a possible sublime than the difficulty of finding fulfillment in a natural world. The frequent use of "or" in the poem indicates the continual falling away of such possibilities:

> Or if the air will not permit,
> Some still removèd place will fit;
> But, O sad Virgin, that thy power
> Might raise Musaeus from his bower,
> Or bid the soul of Orpheus sing
> . . . .
> Or call up him that left half told
> The story of Cambuscan bold.
>
> [ll. 103–05, 109–11]

Brisman observes that "and" may "signal a suspect desire to hold on to the fullness in the fallen world." [18] "Or" seems to acknowledge the inability of that fullness—which is genuinely rich and compelling—to satisfy what Penseroso calls the "fixèd mind," a mind that like Satan's [19] is not to be changed by place or time, but without the full baggage of self-irony that Satan carries. Penseroso turns to the consolations of silence and contemplation, which offer the possibility of the present becoming discontinuous with the past and so comprising a moment of origin that, as Shelley says, mirrors in itself the shadows of futurity.

> Or let my lamp at midnight hour
> Be seen in some high lonely tower,
> Where I may oft outwatch the Bear,
> With thrice great Hermes, or unsphere
> The spirit of Plato to unfold
> What worlds or what vast regions hold
> The immortal mind that hath forsook
> Her mansion in this fleshly nook.
>
> [ll. 85–92]

Penseroso desires an intellectual and anti-natural completion in which self is dissolved and in its ecstasy is granted a deeper vision or new way of seeing: "Dissolve me into ecstasies," he implores, "And bring all heaven before mine eyes" (ll.165–66). Yeats seems wrong to think that only natural existence requires surrender, for the dissolution that is a part of ecstasy implies its own surrender, though perhaps an unconscious one.

The difference between the satisfactions of *L'Allegro* and *Il Penseroso* is from one view the difference between sublimation and repression. This is perhaps an unexpected judgment: is it not Penseroso who, in his renunciation of the natural sphere and his invocation of what Yeats would call an *antithetical* vision, manages to sublimate the instinctual trend we find represented in *L'Allegro?* Sublimation is not, however, a renunciation. It is a new path, a "way out" as Freud says, by which an inhibited desire achieves an acceptable form.²⁰ The beautiful and heart-easing satisfactions of *L'Allegro* are restorative in the sense that they restore the expression of an earlier desire; the vision of *Il Penseroso,* founded on a strong denial, properly depicts repression as Freud understood it. Here Freud and Yeats, whose thoughts on movements of mind are not always congruent, are in general agreement. Yeats finds natural satisfaction, even sublimated to poems, to be *"compensatory"; antithetical* visions, he believes, represent an *"opposed virtue"*—an opposition that seems to imply the repression of what is opposed.²¹

Milton came to regard natural compensation with misgivings similar to those of Yeats. One reason for his later reluctance to embrace the vision of *L'Allegro* is implied in what he must have believed was a necessary dialogue between poet and divinity, or self and other as I have generalized the terms. We meet this relationship so frequently in Milton that readers of his poetry will not need reminders of it. But let us glance at an early expression, in *At a Solemn Music* (1633), of the relation between self and a highly valued otherness:

> With those just Spirits that wear victorious Palms,
> Hymns devout and holy Psalms
> Sing everlastingly;
> That we on earth with undiscording voice
> May rightly answer that melodious noise.

[ll. 14–18]

The speaker could not make proper "answer," and so once more become a part of a "perfect Diapason" (l. 23) that mingles self with otherness in a pure sway of melody, without assuming a voice that is harmonious with that heavenly "noise." Diapason is true correspondence, and as long as the poet conceives otherness as divinity, which in fact it always is in part, his song must be antithetical. Without the choice of an opposed virtue, the other will not be summoned, as we see in *Comus,* a poem in which the Attendant Spirit proclaims the rewards of such a choice:

> Mortals that would follow me,
> Love Virtue, she alone is free;
> She can teach ye how to climb
> Higher than the spherey chime.
> Or if Virtue feeble were,
> Heaven itself would stoop to her.
>
> [ll. 1018–23]

We should set this freedom against the compensatory freedom of *L'Allegro,* which is represented in the later poem by Comus himself. Comus's assumption throughout the poem is that, because the soul is already trapped in mere bodiliness, the higher satisfactions of the Spirit's "Virtue" are impossible, and the self would do well to clothe itself in the delight of sensual bliss. This deep belief is momentarily threatened by the Lady's song, which forces Comus to seek comfort in his remembrance of some earlier singers:

> I have oft heard
> My mother Circe with the Sirens three,
> Amidst the flowery-kirtled Naiades,
> Culling their potent herbs and baleful drugs,
> Who as they sung would take the prisoned soul
> And lap it in Elysium.
>
> [ll. 252–57]

This beautiful reminiscence is an example of what Hartman, taking the term from *Lycidas,* calls "surmise"—a moment of ease that interrupts the poem's progress to a higher truth.[22] Like the catalogue of flowers in *Lycidas,* Comus's remembrance piles sweet on sweet, extending each part of the description, and so prolonging the surmise that what is being

described is as compelling as the difficult truth that evoked
it. Thus we are not merely told of the Sirens but told they
were stationed "Amidst the flowery-kirtled Naiades"; and
they were not only singing, but culling their herbs as well.
The description opens into itself and creates a pause that for
the moment denies the opposed power of the Lady's song—
or Edward King's death, in *Lycidas*.

In *Lycidas* the surmise is abruptly broken by the swain's
recognition that he has been dreaming only, that the fiction
of the flowers cannot console; and so he bids farewell to all
"ease": "For so to interpose a little ease / Let our frail
thoughts dally with false surmise" (ll.152–53). Comus, too,
becomes aware that Circe and the Sirens merely dallied with
the self and that the Lady's song reflects a "waking bliss."

> Yet they in pleasing slumber lulled the sense,
> And in sweet madness robbed it of itself;
> But such a sacred and home-felt delight,
> Such sober certainty of waking bliss,
> I never heard till now.
>
> [ll. 260–64]

If Comus could make her "sober certainty" his own, he in
effect could complete a perfect diapason with a response of
true consent. But though he knows she wakes while he
sleeps, his response implies the belief that the soul is imprisoned irremediably. Consequently, his surmise depends for
its compellingness on a turn into the self that is also a turn
away from her higher truth: his is the pleasure of isolated
selfhood, where the self withdraws from all outer things to
be lapped in an Elysium that holds out no hope—much less
certainty—for the soul's life.

Comus's Elysium is the seat of a blissful suffusion much
like Warton's, in which self is compensated for a failed futurity. He offers the Lady, now imprisoned like the soul
lapped by Circe, a happiness of the body and of natural
plenitude, in which a great horizontal profusion takes the
place of a possible ascent:

> Wherefore did Nature pour her bounties forth
> With such a full and unwithdrawing hand,
> Covering the earth with odours, fruits, and flocks
> Thronging the seas with spawn innumerable,
> But all to please and sate the curious taste?
>
> [ll. 710–14]

The Lady does not allow herself to be "lapped," of course. She argues for moderation and the universal distribution of Nature's bounty, and for the virtue of chastity. But she might have argued against Comus's hypothesis as well as his thesis, for his aggrandizement of "ease" is based on an assumption of human frailty that the Lady is bound to reject.

> Scorning the unexempt condition
> By which all mortal frailty must subsist,
> Refreshment after toil, ease after pain,
> That have been tired all day without repast,
> And timely rest have wanted.
>
> [ll. 685–89]

Comus's "ease after pain" clearly echoes the deathly advice of Spenser's Despair to the Red Cross Knight. Despair, in lines Milton remembered, tries to make the Knight his own by persuading him that "Sleepe after toyle, port after stormie seas, / Ease after warre, death after life does greatly please" (*The Faerie Queene*, I, ix, 40). Those who "have been tired all day" need "timely rest," Comus urges the Lady. This sounds like the just reward of "port after stormie seas," but *Comus* makes consistent use of musical metaphors. What the sorcerer actually offers is silence—a "rest" in the musical sense of a silent interval—and so the stasis of death.

Here we may have one reason for Milton's ambivalence toward surmise. Natural or sensual bliss delights in profusion, as Yeats says, but to choose this mode is to pause and so risk a death that is death-in-life. Hence the characteristic syntactic construction of those moments of surmise in Milton's poetry, that add layer to layer—but in a direction perpendicular to the higher mood of the poem. Milton is a poet who is intensely aware of proper relationship, of mutual discourse between self and other; but surmise silences that hoped for dialogue because it represents a self-involvement that denies otherness, which to the poet is the only life, however antithetical. In Milton one cannot compensate for "mortal frailty," one can only oppose it.

If we proceed one step further we see that freedom in Milton is a close kin of denial. This association is also urged on us by the Attendant Spirit who, like Comus, is ravished by the Lady's song.

> At last a soft and solemn-breathing sound
> Rose like a steam of rich distilled perfumes,
> And stole upon the air, that even Silence
> Was took ere she was ware, and wished she might
> Deny her nature and be never more,
> Still to be so displaced. I was all ear,
> And took in strains that might create a soul
> Under the ribs of Death.
>
>   [ll. 555–62]

Whereas Comus turns from the thought of frailty, the Spirit acknowledges Death as the terminus of continuity. The Lady's song rises like Penseroso and images a possible life by subsuming Silence. The Spirit makes no promises (as Spirit he does not have need of these; his words are intended to instruct the brothers): those strains "might" create a soul under Death's ribs. The only certainty in the lines is that the ribs do belong to Death. A possibility is that communication with the music that approximates heavenly music—"I was all ear"—may bring the self to otherness and from that encounter create life from death.

This order of life is, however, antithetical: it derives from a form of renunciation that is characteristic of the anti-natural strain in poetry. And it has as one of its goals a "freedom" that Milton counterposes to Comus's acceptance of the soul's imprisonment. Here even the Attendant Spirit momentarily falters, for when he comes upon the Lady frozen to marble by Comus, he voices the fear that "We cannot free" her without reversing Comus's rod. But her immobility is not rest; freedom for her is of another order, as she says earlier to Comus:

> Thou canst not touch the freedom of my mind
> With all thy charms, although this corporeal rind
> Thou hast immanacl'd.

[ll. 663–65]

Comus's "charms" are those of Circe's cup and wand—the emblems of a compulsion to repeat instinctual satisfactions. One senses Milton's quite genuine dualism in the separation between these pleasures and the opposed freedom of mind which seeks countercharms to them. Both Comus and the Lady appear to be reacting to an awareness of fall (in this sense, perhaps both their rituals should be thought of as countercharms), and this seems a prior condition for both the natural and anti-natural modes: but Comus is fated to reiterate, whereas the Lady seeks discontinuity. For this reason the poem is as good an example of Yeats's opposed categories of "primary" or "emotional," and "antithetical" or "intellectual" as we shall find.

Hartman, an invaluable guide to the history of surmise, thought the Romantic enterprise might be viewed as an effort to make surmise seem truthful, rather than false.[23] How true was it for Milton? The question would seem to be answered by the swain's complaint in *Lycidas* of its falseness. But the Romantics usually detected a sympathy on Milton's part for those easeful passages. So Keats claims in his annotations to *Paradise Lost* that Milton "had an exquisite passion for what is properly in the sense of ease and pleasure, poetical Luxury." [24] Nor can one help but feel that passion, as it evokes moments in which the heart is comforted by an exquisite dallying. Nevertheless, we underestimate Milton's commitment to the antithetical sublime, which is merely another way of saying "opposed virtue," if we regard these as the true loci of his sympathy. (On the other hand, we may very well read statements such as Keats's as self-commentaries.) "The passions, when we know that they cannot find fulfillment, become vision," Yeats writes.[25] Milton seems to have felt that the fulfillment of those passions is a form of death, and in those passages we label surmise, he bids farewell to ease and luxury with the nostalgia of the antithetical poet, who may have difficulty taking his leave but has a sense that he is going on to embrace his destiny. To do otherwise, for Milton, is to risk losing poetic voice by being "taken" by a higher strain (as Silence is), or to lose poetic identity before the mellowing year grants it, as he says in *Lycidas*.

This "sober certainty" enables Milton to pass the bowers of bliss unalarmed, knowing they contain "charms" that enthrall or captivate in the root meaning of these terms, by which one is chained as well as delighted. Keats, as I imply in my Preface, will evolve an oxymoronic response to otherness; Milton usually uses oxymorons only as ironic comments on Satan, who struggles against an other who is absolute. Milton, that is, is an "either/or" poet, and it is this terrible weight of the necessity of choice (rather than the possibility of reconciliation) that he passes on to later poets. Yeats, who at his most antithetical approximates a Miltonic severity, believes that "the Daemon brings us to the place of choice," forcing us to choose *between* the primary and the antithetical. If we take the paradigm of the ego's dependent relations as a commentary on this choice, the individual chooses either instinctual satisfaction or the dictates of super-ego as the means of self-completion.

For a poet such as Collins, however, the power manifested in otherness is irreconcilable, and the desire for closure remains hauntingly unsatisfied. A number of excellent commentaries have been written on Collins's *Ode on the Poetical Character,* which critics now tend to view as a precursor to the Romantic ode.[26] One point of central interest in the poem is the portrayal of the poet's relation to past poets—especially Milton, who in the poem becomes the daemon of exclusion for all later poets. This is an overtly pessimistic view of the possibility of the poet's subsuming otherness; and indeed the poem may be read as a quest for possession, in which the poet seeks to introject what seems almost literally to belong to his precursor. Only an Apollo-figure like the Youth of Morn, who unites inner and outer, can be said to possess otherness: "And thou, thou rich-haired Youth of Morn, / And all thy subject life was born." Life itself is "subject" to the Youth, whose wholeness or completion evaporates differences between self and otherness.

Pure relation such as this obviates the possibility of oxymoron or irony, which is born when division intrudes upon poetic hope. "Where is the bard," Collins asks without expecting a reply (one can imagine Milton voicing the question as prelude to a "higher" response from a divine power), "whose soul can now / Its high presuming hopes avow? / Where he who thinks, with rapture blind, / This hallow'd work for him designed?" Loss of relation has occurred in the time since the Youth of Morn. What poet can now possess the world? The question might be phrased, What form of subjectivity can compensate for object-loss? or, How does one achieve Unity of Being? For the ideal Collins sets out is a "rapture blind" in which the poetic consciousness, however blind to external things, becomes a form of self-possession that enables the poet to reassume his feeling that what is outside is subject to his power.

The exemplar of blind rapture is Milton, for the poet's paradise is "an Eden like his own." The point of this particular possession is clear: Milton's Eden is the place of rendezvous, where he hears the "native strains" of Heaven. Those strains are not only indigenous but suggest as well Milton's own nativity (the Latin *nasci*) as Heaven's true son, a poet in the line of the Apollonian "Youth":

> I view that oak, the fancied glades among,
> By which as Milton lay, his ev'ning ear,
> From many a cloud that drop'd ethereal dew,
> Nigh spher'd in Heav'n its native strains could hear:
> On which that ancient trump he reach'd was hung.
>
> [ll. 63–67]

"Native" usually suggests origins in Milton, and Collins, as readers know, is suffused with Milton's own diction. When in *Paradise Lost* the rebel angels begin war in heaven, they threaten to "disturb, / Though not destroy, their happy native seat" (VI, 225–26); and when Adam laments the gravest consequence of his fall, he asks, "But have I now seen Death? Is this the way / I must return to native dust?" (XI, 462–63). The "strains" Milton hears are born in heaven, but by creating the "jealous steep" of Eden he touches himself with a new birth. The poet may be blind in his rapture, but as in a frequent Romantic substitution of sense, he *hears* what is lost to others and makes gain of necessary loss.

Thus Milton raises the meeting soul to otherness. But Milton himself is the other to Collins, who can only "view" Milton's "oak" and "fancied glades" (for Collins, "desired" as well as creations of "fancy") and then make a vain attempt to "greet" Milton's glory.

> Thither oft, his glory greeting,
> From Waller's myrtle shades retreating,
> With many a vow from Hope's aspiring tongue,
> My trembling feet his guiding steps pursue;
> In vain.
>
> [ll. 68–72]

Collins's "greeting" is almost an invocation proper, a renunciation of the false words of Waller and a deep expression of homage to Milton. Poetic desire lies behind this homage; the self is subjugated as a greatly desired identity is reached after. For Collins this is a highly serious quest, one which we may view as a form of love. It may be just the magnitude of Collins's devotion, however, that ironically contributes to his unhappy exclusion from that sense of identity and makes Milton appear as daemon. In his devotion, Collins displaces love to his idea of Milton, which he then hopes to embrace. Freud interprets such displacements as concealed forms of narcissism: what we lack we love in another, and by loving the other we try to possess again the love we cannot bestow upon ourselves. This is the process that Freud calls *idealization;* in it, "the object is being treated in the same way as our own ego . . ."; or "the object serves as a substitute for some unattained ego ideal of our own."

> We love it on account of the perfections which we have
> striven to reach for our own ego, and which we should
> now like to procure in this roundabout way as a means
> of satisfying our narcissism.[27]

Freud thinks of this attitude toward the object as an overvaluation—such feelings may be necessary to our love of self,
but they are inconsistent with reality—which, if it continues,
makes the object become "more and more sublime and precious, until at last it gets possession of the entire self-love of
the ego, whose self-sacrifice thus follows as a natural consequence." What the later poet hoped to possess now, in a
manner of speaking, possesses him. And it is at this point
that a profound psychological substitution occurs, one which
is a direct consequence of devotion. "The whole situation
can be completely summarized in a formula," Freud con-
cludes: *"the object has been put in the place of the ego ideal."* [28] In
this manner the precursor whose identity is sought to complete the self becomes a power that threatens the self as the
super-ego may threaten the ego with fear of separation.

Here we have a profound irony and one of the great dilemmas of the subjective poet: he believes his quest for
wholeness or completion will lead him to (or back to) that
enchanted ground that shelters divinity, perhaps his own
earlier divinity: in the subjective poet's nostalgic longings for
presence there is a Youth of Morn. But in the daemonic
form, the quest may lead (if unsuccessful), not to a power
that seems beneficent, but to the poet's feeling that he is
condemned to a region outside what he sees as his proper
domain. On a subjective level, Freud's view of emotional development describes an attempt to recover an earlier inte-
grated self not unlike the self that is blind with "rapture" in
Collins. "The development of the ego," Freud writes, "consists in a departure from primary narcissim and gives rise to
a vigorous attempt to recover that state." When the poet
seeks completion of his quest, however, he discovers that the
muse or power is no longer the id, which the ego would
satisfy if it could, *but the superego,* which rejects the ego and,
in the form of a great precursor or the powers of destiny,

stubbornly maintains a division the poet hoped to heal. The "departure" experienced by the ego in its development, according to Freud, "is brought about by means of the displacement of libido on to an ego ideal imposed from without. . . ." [29] But if the ego ideal or super-ego abandons the ego, the poet tends to give up in despair the hope of a successful conclusion to the quest: the quest, in fact, sometimes seems to be undertaken precisely so that the poet *can* fail. As the poem concludes, then, Collins's separation from Milton's poetical character becomes a form of inner division, and the past assumes the posture of that satanic outsidedness that one finds so often in Thomas Gray as well:

> My trembling feet his guiding steps pursue;
> In vain—such bliss to one alone,
> Of all the sons of soul was known,
> And Heaven, and Fancy, kindred powers,
>   Have now o'erturned the inspiring bowers,
> Or curtain'd close such scene from every future view.
>   [ll. 71–76]

The Two Beams of the Cross

Are all poetic encounters with the sublimity of otherness, then, only attempts to renew a vanished self-love? Probably the question should be divided into its components: first, Is the poet's attempt to "greet" the daemonic power merely a way of satisfying the ego ideal? and second, Is the contrary effort to marry a softer, more benignant power—Collins's Pity or Mercy, say—an approach to narcissism by its alternate route, through the emotions that compensate for object-loss? Freud is quite insistent that the departure from narcissism comes about in only one of two ways: by the development of the super-ego, which brings to an end the "happy" state of primary narcissism, and by the individual's inevitable attachments to "objects"—people and ideas, as well as things—in the outer world. Moreover, though we need to feel on our pulses, as Keats would say, that Freud is right before we can accept his conceptualization, we cannot dis-

pense with narcissism merely because it seems to reduce poetry and even perhaps to denigrate it. After all, what is being
denigrated may be only our own "over-valuation" of poetry,
which, Freud might deftly propose, is a consequence of our
own narcissism as readers. Finally, *On Narcissism: An Introduction* is a cornerstone of Freud's monumental theory
and provides him with an explanation for human motivation. Strachey, Freud's great editor and translator, implicitly
warns against easy dismissal, for he regards the paper as
"among the most important of Freud's writings," and believes it should "be regarded as one of the pivots in the
evolution of his views." [30]

Let us begin an answer by examining one of Freud's own
crucial assumptions—that the reality-principle forces the
reasonable observer to regard imagination as neurotic
error—and then proceed to some considerations of poetic
encounters with an apparent otherness. Freud's ambivalence
to artistic creativity is well known. While holding in highest
regard the depth of insight of writers, he tended to group
artists with primitive men and neurotics, for he felt that each
of these overvalues the power of thought. "Thought" (which
shades into animism) and "reality" (which is comprehended
by science) become two terms of an opposition that is central
to Freud's views of neurosis and the emotional development
of the individual. Thus for primitives, neurotics, and artists,
a "general overvaluation" has come about "of all mental processes—an attitude towards the world, that is, which in view
of our knowledge of the relation between reality and
thought, cannot fail to strike *us* as an overvaluation of the
latter." [31] To underscore the frailty of belief in what he calls
"the omnipotence of thought," he notes that the "scientific
view of the universe no longer affords any room for human
omnipotence; men have acknowledged their smallness and
submitted resignedly to death and to the other necessities of
nature." [32] The opposition therefore centers upon how
much truth one can accept—whether the individual resigns
himself to a final and overpowering reality or seeks the false
magic of the mind.

Freud is able to relate this distinction to narcissism and,

significantly, implies the basis for the individual's propensity toward narcissistic thinking. Any *"over-*valuation" of psychical acts, he writes, "may plausibly be brought into relation with narcissism and regarded as an essential component of it." Belief in the power of thoughts goes along with an "unshakable confidence in the possibility of controlling the world"—a form of magic, that is—and "the principle governing magic, the technique of the animistic mode of thinking, is the principle of the 'omnipotence of thoughts.' " [33] Magic, then, which for Freud would include artistic creation, is in the service of narcissism and is intended to exert a measure of control over the outward reality that Freud himself would urge us to accept as omnipotent. The "acts" of neurotics (and we recall here Freud's statement that "in only a single field of our civilization has the omnipotence of thoughts been retained, and that is in the field of art"),[34] Freud therefore concludes, "are of an entirely magical character. If they are not charms, they are at all events counter-charms, designed to ward off . . . expectations of disaster. . . . Whenever I have succeeded in penetrating the mystery, I have found that the expected disaster was death." [35] This statement is consistent with his later view, contained in the essay *On Narcissism,* that "the most touchy point" in the entire narcissistic system is "the immortality of the ego, which is so hard pressed by reality. . . ." [36] The necessity of preserving this idea of immortality appears to be the basis of narcissistic thinking: it is a ritual mode that serves to defend the self against the power of negation (at the hands of reality) and so evidence intimations of immortality.

There is some correspondence between Freud's concept and the workings of a number of poems since Milton. The question for us as readers is, Does narcissism therefore define the limits of poetic quests? or, in Burke's description, Are we involved in the imagery of a poem because we find our own desires for self-satisfaction realized? We will return to this variation on our original question. We should note first, if briefly, that poems of self-inauguration, or the announcement of a truth with which the poet identifies himself, may indeed follow Freud's formulation of ritual. Milton's *On the Morning of Christ's Nativity,* which Kenneth Allott has shown is the source of Keats's *Ode to Psyche,*[37] charms (or countercharms) into silence all oracles that proclaim the omnipotence of truths other than God's (and the poet's) own: "The oracles are dumb, / No voice or hideous hum / Runs through the arched roof in words deceiving." It is at this point in poems treating the discovery of true identity, when every opposing daemon of the tradition has been silenced, that the poet proclaims his own word, every true godhead corresponding in part to himself as poet: "Our Babe, to show his Godhead true, / Can in his swaddling bands control the damned crew." The divinity of proper godhead is a legitimate poetic quest-object (whether achieved or not): the poet counters the deceiving words of the truths of necessity in hope of arriving at the point of "control," which is a power if not a magic.

This ritualistic assertion of one's own possible omnipotence need not imply solipsism however, any more than Freud's own theorizing. Freud himself seems to have wished not to be surprised by sin, where sin is the equivalent of psychic overvaluation. Any reconciliation between the "thought" of an idealistic poet and the "reality" of an objective psychoanalyst must be difficult. Before hazarding preliminary replies to questions that demand finalities, we may observe that Freud's view of his *own* emotional and psychological development suggests that the objectivity of his "science" was perhaps as much an idea or ideal as the verbal structures of poets, no matter how subjective. Freud's model of development includes three phases: narcissism, object-choice, and a third stage which he calls "the scientific phase," in which "an individual has reached maturity, has renounced the pleasure principle, adjusted himself to reality and turned to the external world for the object of his desires."[38] This last description might almost be taken as the goal of all therapy, though Freud intends it only as a proper demonstration of the link between science and "maturity." Yet if we turn to a later work, the "Postscript" (1935) to *An Autobiographical*

Study, we see that Freud believed that he never achieved that final stage of development:

> since I put forward my hypothesis of the existence of two classes of instinct (Eros and the death instinct) and since I proposed a division of the mental personality into an ego, a super-ego, and an id, I have made no further decisive contributions to psycho-analysis: what I have written on the subject since then has been either unessential or would soon have been supplied by someone else. This circumstance is connected with an alteration in myself, with what might be described as a phase of regressive development. My interest, after making a lifelong *détour* through the natural sciences, medicine and psychotherapy, returned to the cultural problems which had fascinated me long before, when I was a youth scarcely old enough for thinking.[39]

One thinks of Ernest Jones's belief that Freud always cared more for proper understanding than for therapy, and of Freud's essay on Leonardo, which tries to come to terms with the reasons for which the great artist left art for scientific research, only to return late in life to his art; and one wonders whether the statement of a narcist-evading "scientific phase" is not merely a hope voiced from the partial perspective of a *détour*. For Freud's severe theory similarly cannot comprehend a third or synthesizing stage: the choice is either/or, either repression or sublimation, id or super-ego, omnipotence of thought or truth of reality.

A more accurate view of poets might find not a regression but a return that seeks to join difficult contraries. Geoffrey Hartman, trying to reconcile Freud with a "psychogenetic theory of figurative thinking," notes the "paradox" of the persistence of idealism in the face of empiricism. "And as a kind of realism—the realism of the solipsist—it will never be dislodged but will continue to nourish our skepticism vis-à-vis a true or decisive contact with 'reality.' "[40] I would like to take Professor Hartman's suggestion of a paradox at the heart of the poetic encounter, though I see other elements at the core. The question of thought or idealism versus reality at first seems to be one of communication: does our thought (or the poet's) communicate at all with something outside, or do we, and does he, merely court a false omnipotence? Burke, who proposed communication as a solution to the problem, finally believed that a proper resolution needed to be formulated in terms of libido, as we have seen.

But let us follow Burke further and attempt to view the central problem of self and other, poet and "text" as a problem of libido or love, in which resolution involves the intermingling of contraries. The final and fullest relationship of poet to other is paradoxical in the sense that it is oxymoronic: the poet speaks from a point at the edge of ego, as it were, a border of self that touches otherness, and he seems to both go out from himself and retain selfhood. The statement of this relationship—which I will explain more fully—is "final" because subjective poets do not seem to achieve it without earlier passing through a series of ambivalent relations with otherness, before learning, first, that the other cannot be approached without loss to the self, and second, that the other can be possessed most completely by holding the self open to that loss. This point, the goal of some of our greatest "subjective" poems—Shelley's *Ode to the West Wind,* Keats's *The Fall of Hyperion,* Yeats's *The Man and the Echo*—is not precisely Freud's warding off disaster, nor is it wholly narcissistic self-satisfaction. It is better seen as self-completion or wholeness, though its emotional dimension includes forgiveness, as Yeats suggests in *A Dialogue of Self and Soul;* for as we have seen in the ode *Ode on the Poetical Character,* the daemon of otherness is often a power that isolates the poet and deprives him of the capacity to be self-forgiving.

I want to suggest, then, that one essential distinction between the Romantic enterprise and that of either Freud or Milton can be seen in the later poets' efforts to find and remain at a border of existence at which contrary spheres of existence—emotion and intellect, narcissism and object-love, self-investment and ecstasy—are neither opposed (as in Mil-

ton and Freud) nor juxtaposed (as in much of Yeats) but
joined in a tenuous relationship that often is expressed ox-
ymoronically. We can see the partial statement of this in
Hazlitt's comment on the fallen angels, which I have used as
part of this book's epigraph. Hazlitt, so like the Romantics in
this respect, aggrandizes the fallen state as Milton represents
it because in it only does he find a possible mingling of an
emotional "pathos" and ecstatic "sublimity." Keats, in the
second part of the epigraph, carries Hazlitt's "mingled" contraries to their logical rhetorical conclusion, in the powerful
oxymoron of "the sublime pathetic"—which captures opposed tendencies in a single representation.

Since there are corresponding emotional—what Coleridge
might call "moral"—dimensions to the rhetorical device of
the oxymoron, I do not think we can dismiss it as merely a
poetic fiction. The complete satisfaction of either an instinctual need or the demand of an ego ideal—this may reach
toward fiction. But the joining that rhetorically seems to be a
synthesis is more accurately thought of, I believe, as a reconciliation: some need, some wish or desire is met by the failure of otherness to satisfy or answer, and the poet's response
is to both love and forgive that outerness, and so necessarily
to be self-forgiving. Burke says that the poet's word tends to
name the object emotionally—"vindictively, or plaintively,"
and so on. Perhaps we can venture that, in the climax of the
encounter with the power he summons, the poet names *for-
givingly,* in a form of love that is turned outward even as it
reaches inward.

The elaboration of this relation will occupy the succeeding
chapters, but let us consider a statement by Yeats in which a
scene that is the equivalent of Collins's "inspiring bowers" is
presented as a trysting place where the contraries that are
crucial to poetic origins meet:

> the nobleness of the Arts is in the mingling of con-
> traries, the extremity of sorrow, the extremity of joy,
> perfection of personality, the perfection of its surren-
> der, overflowing turbulent energy, and marmorean still-

> ness; and its red rose opens at the meeting of the two
> beams of the cross, and at the trysting-place of mortal
> and immortal, time and eternity.[41]

Yeats images a place in which the poet realizes Collins's unsuccessful "greeting" of Milton's spirit, a place where "personality" is both achieved and surrendered to the power of the
other. All relations to externality have this potential, yet poetic development usually consists in a period of surrender
followed by one of a more isolated and defiant personality;
only in a third phase, quite unlike Freud's curiously monistic
"scientific" phase, do we find Yeats's statement to be appli-
cable. Yeats may be anticipating not only his own development (or perhaps his critics) but his theory of the daemon,
that encompassing other whose threat moves the poet to difficult accomplishment. For the "beams of the cross" may be
seen as the upwardness of the daemonic other and the horizontal of the natural self, or primary man. Only where self
meets other does the rose that is poetry grow, for at this
border of existence we have entered the point of rendezvous, where the poet greets all that is "immortal," the outerness that he comes to both love and fear. He could not
enact that greeting without the semblance of sacrifice, the
threat of the crucifixion of the self; but the reward is to
achieve a proper poetic self that incorporates the power of
otherness. Milton seems largely to have escaped the necessity
of oxymoron in this encounter, for an *unambivalent* "love"
for the Attendant Spirit's "virtue" tends to make an identity
of poetic self and supreme other. Though it is probably true
that many poets through the Romantics saw Milton speaking
in the Spirit's final lines—"Mortals that would follow me
. . ."—and tried to follow accordingly, none could achieve
the semblance of that identity without mingling Yeats's contraries.

Yeats, following Nietzsche, uses the term "antithetical" for
the anti-natural imagination, which is intellectual, and opposes this to the primary self, which is emotional. Where
Milton largely removes ambivalence from the antithetical (or

seemed to have for those who followed), poets since him
have had to acknowledge that the antithetical other whom
they address as "Thou" (in its various forms) has a degree of
power over them, in part because they have idealized it. The
wish for "poetic character" is a wish for identity, and to see it
in another (as seems inevitable) is to grant that other not
only power but a measure of self-love. If this sounds suspi-
ciously like Freud's formula for the ego confronting the
super-ego as it is projected onto an external object, it is, for
this is the first term of the oxymoron. To open oneself out to
that power, as Keats does with Moneta in *The Fall of Hyperion,* is the second term and brings the poet *past* the renewed narcissism of Freud to a state of vision, the unfolding
of the rose. Here primary meets antithetical, and the poet
seems to transcend subjectivity, settling for neither a com-
pensating emotion nor the antithetical sublime but a fusion,
however brief, in which emotion and intellect are united.
During this moment the poet achieves the paradoxical state
that Yeats thinks of as being "self-possessed in self-surrender," a recognition that, ironically, self is only whole when it
surrenders to other.

Nearly always, the other, though approached by the
youthful poet as beneficent, returns to the mature poet as
threatening—more or less like Freud's super-ego. This is not
merely a formula but a dimension of the profound experience of the mature poet: Shelley's Wind, Keats's Nightingale
and muse-goddesses, Yeats's Soul and Echo all demand the
death of the poet, in one way or another. Their sublimity
must be humanized, though such humanizations always lead
to loss before a final (and frail) gain. We become less a part
of the imagery in poems of this type than the sympathetic
audience that sees its fate in another's. The poet's victory,
though terribly won and often diminished, is also ours, and
though there may be ambivalence here, our proper role as
readers must be to open ourselves out to the poem, which
for us is the other. Though one step removed, reading
requires a surrender not unlike the poet's own, and a

reader's subsequent response (his intellection of the experience) is the second term of the oxymoron.

It is apparent that my concern is not with the relation of
poet to "nature" so much as with his idea of a power outside
himself that motivates his writing—what we ordinarily call
the muse, though the Romantics usually address it as a form
of beauty. Encounters with that beauty progress from idealization and self-surrender to internalization and finally to a
marriage of inner and outer. Wallace Stevens conceives this
mingling of contraries much as Yeats does, though his presentation of it in *Notes Toward a Supreme Fiction* suggests that
trysts yield a "change" that may be a point of origination:

> Two things of opposite natures seem to depend
> On one another, as a man depends
> On a woman, day on night, the imagined
>
> On the real. This is the origin of change.
> Winter and spring, cold copulars, embrace
> And forth the particulars of rapture come.

A number of Romantic quests have as their object such as
"embrace," and though often it is not achieved, or only
partly achieved—so that the poet, like Keats's "knight-at-
arms" in *La Belle Dame Sans Merci,* ends alone on a cold hill-
side—when the embrace is complete it expresses the fullness
of a love that encompasses both self and other, subject and
object, emotional being and the idea of the perfect; and
from that love "the particulars of rapture come."

2

Keats: The Poet's Eye

> It is hard to become a mere hand and ear. Did the first
> [poet] of us all hate the blindness that kept him from
> the oblivion of activity?
>
> Yeats, *Memoirs*

If the poet's embrace of an ambivalent other can reconcile indeed the opposed trends of primary emotion and antithetical intellection, it does so only after considerable poetic development. Poets at the outset tend to idealize the prospect before them, as Wordsworth observes in *Resolution and Independence:* "We Poets in our youth begin in gladness," he writes, though he adds that in the end there may come despondency. In his early gladness a poet may idealize either the emotional (as Wordsworth did) or the antithetical (as Yeats did); or he may see no intrinsic reason why the two cannot be brought together easily. Keats essentially follows Wordworth in at first aggrandizing the emotional sphere, and though he feels some attraction to Apollo and the sublime, the center of the poems tends to focus on the possibilities of renewal rather than renunciation.

Keats published his first volume, *Poems, 1817,* against the well-meant advice of Shelley, who was three years his senior, and despite some difficulty in providing a sufficient number of poems to justify a volume. He was eager to announce himself as an English poet, and the poems he included (which amounted to nearly all he had written) ring with the praises of the craft and of Poesy, the shaping spirit who serves as his muse in his major effort, *Sleep and Poetry.* The poems tend to be optimistic, expectant, and even, by identification with the tradition, proud. But just before the volume went to press Keats quickly penned a dedicatory sonnet to Leigh Hunt that seems to be of another mood:

> Glory and loveliness have passed away,
> For if we wander out in early morn
> No wreathèd incense do we see upborne
> Into the east, to meet the smiling day;
> No crowd of nymphs soft-voiced and young and gay,
> In woven baskets bringing ears of corn,
> Roses and pinks and violets to adorn
> The shrine of Flora on her early May.

The form of Keats's complaint, that glory and loveliness have departed, probably comes from Wordsworth: the *Intimations* ode laments in similar terms the poet's sense that "there hath past away a glory from the earth" (ll.18). Departed glories make sense as introductions to first volumes if they make possible the young poet's claim that he can restore them, which is essentially what we learn in the sestet of the sonnet. "There are left delights as high as these," Keats asserts—with the implication that he will go on to sing of them, and so inaugurate their return.

Because it was written just after the poems included in the volume, the dedicatory sonnet tends to reiterate their concerns (or anticipate them, if read in Keats's ordering).⁹ It is significant, therefore, that the sonnet construes restoration as the poet's task, or rather as his privilege, for Keats blesses his "destiny" that there are "delights" that yet remain to him. Several of the more important poems in *1817*—the verse epistles *To George Felton Mathew* and *To my Brother George,* and *I Stood Tip-toe*—have as one of their objects the demonstration of the possibilities of return, whereby glory and loveliness are seen to be still accessible. But it is the idea of return (rather than its validity) that should concern us. In his ode (which also greatly influenced the *Hymn to Intellectual Beauty,* Shelley's poem of poetic self-discovery) Wordsworth does speak "of something that is gone," but he knows that what he has lost is "for ever taken from my sight" (ll. 53,

177). There can be no return of what the poet has loved, only the greater love that attends the knowledge of mortality, and the eye that watches over it.

The plots of Keats's early poems, on the contrary, trace restorations that deny the permanence of departure. This possibility of *L'Allegro* obtains in the verse epistle to his brother George and in *I Stood Tip-toe,* among other poems in the volume. Thus, although the sonnet to Hunt on a literal level complains that "glory and loveliness" have fled, the epistle declares that "the poet's eye can reach those golden halls, / And view the glory of their festivals" (ll. 35–36). Similarly, the moon (the muse) in *I Stood Tip-toe* is the "closer of lovely eyes to lovely dreams" and Keats recognizes that "Thee must I praise above all other glories" (ll.120, 123). The poet's eye can see, and what he sees is a world renovated, one which he can love. Another way of viewing this renovation is to recognize that the complaint for lost glory and loveliness is part of a rhetorical formula by which the poet prepares the way for the power of his own seeing. In the early poems, we notice that power belongs to the idealized figure of the poet, which our poet only hopes to appropriate.

Renovation is itself part of the larger plot of emotional compensation. In Keats this takes the form of the discovered "wonders" of poetic seeing becoming a cure not only of the ground, as Stevens might say, but of personal loss:

> Ah! could I tell the wonder of an isle
> That in the fairest lake had placèd been,
> I could e'en Dido of her grief beguile,
> Or rob from agèd Lear his bitter teen;
> For sure so fair a place was never seen,
> Of all that ever charmed romantic eye.

This is the *Imitation of Spenser* (ll.19–24), which Charles Brown identifies as Keats's earliest poem, probably written in early 1814. The poet's eye can reach even this enchanted isle, for the conclusion of the poem (ll. 25–36) consists of a full description of those beguiling wonders. Keats's happy idealism here toys with the possibility of the charmed eye dispersing worldly grief, as if faulty seeing went along with the emotional consequences of fallenness. In this formulation we may miss the ambivalences of Keats's mature poetry, but these lines represent an early statement of one of Keats's most consistent and powerful themes, the relation of poetry to consolation. The anguish of those lovers who, like Lear and Dido, cannot love, which has resonance with the poet's own need to love, is what Keats hoped poetry would relieve. The journey through various trials of invention that attempt this relief, and through the expectation, fear, and even guilt that are discovered along the way, is a journey through Keats's poetry and might begin with the major poems of *1817.*

I Stood Tip-toe is a poem that mediates between landscape poetry and something more serious—a poem on the relation of men to gods, and the mythopoeic imagination that attends that relationship. The delicately intermediate approach is implicit in the poet's posture at the outset: he stands amidst the natural delight of lush flora, but he is on "tip-toe," somewhat like the sweetpeas he sees that are "on tip-toe for a flight" to something higher (ll. 57). An exuberant feeling pervades much of the poem, but this slight sense of a poise between worlds forces the reader to question even the rich portraiture that seems to imply a commitment to the natural sphere alone.

For in the air that is "so very still' there lurks a silence that suggests the hidden presence of a spectre of some sort, a genius loci that makes this a more than natural scene:

> The clouds were pure and white as flocks new shorn,
> And fresh from the clear brook; sweetly they slept
> On the blue fields of heaven, and then there crept
> A little noiseless noise among the leaves,
> Born of the very sigh that silence heaves,
> For not the faintest motion could be seen
> Of all the shades that slanted o'er the green.
>
> [ll. 8–14]

Though muted, the presence of the ghost that halts meditation on the natural prospect anticipates the constructions
of mythological explanation that come later in the poem;
and, more darkly, it anticipates the silent landscape of *Hyperion* into which Saturn is plunged once he is disinherited
from those heavens that once were his:

> No stir of air was there,
> Not so much life as on a summer's day
> Robs not one light seed from the feathered grass.
>
> [I, 7–9]

Silence is almost never congenial to natural or primary poetic imaginings in Keats, though it is sometimes made to appear to be so. In *I Stood Tip-toe* the faint presence of otherness leads the poet as if by reflex to greedily ingest the
bounty of the landscape, until the mild threat is absorbed by
a more beneficent mystery, that of origins.

> There was wide wandering for the greediest eye,
> To peer about upon variety;
> Far round the horizon's crystal air to skim,
> And trace the dwindled edgings of its brim;
> To picture out the quaint and curious bending
> Of a fresh woodland alley, never ending;
> Or by the bowery clefts and leafy shelves
> Guess where the jaunty streams refresh themselves.
> I gazed awhile and felt as light and free
> As though the fanning wings of Mercury
> Had played upon my heels.
>
> [ll. 15–25]

Though a fuller statement will have to await our discussion
of *Endymion,* Keats's turn from the ghost in the landscape to
the "greediest eye" is not arbitrary. "Greed" in Keats signals
selfhood, the natural self that opposes daemonic identifications. The "variety" that the "bodily eye" (as Wordsworth
says) seeks is manifold nature, the seeming endlessness of
satisfaction that Milton, to consider momentarily a counter-
voice, found so threatening to true life. When Keats goes on

to skim the horizon "Far round," we should draw a contrast
with the "Far, far around" of the *Ode to Psyche,* in which the
horizon has been internalized, in an attempt to make relationship with otherness possible. In *I Stood Tip-toe* the restorative imaginings are of depth, the "never ending" alley
and the site of the origin of the streams. A prospective reading might note the repetition of "Guess" (*I Stood Tip-toe,* l. 22)
in the *Ode to a Nightingale,* in which Keats stands "in embalmèd darkness" and must therefore "guess each sweet" (l. 43)
that rises from the unseen flowers. Guessing in *Nightingale* is
more complex but introduces (and makes possible) the catalogue of flowers that fills the poet's paradise. The guessing
in *I Stood Tip-toe* makes possible a return to ease that erases
the remembrance of the spectral landscape, which might (if
attended) preclude the poet's delight in the "jaunty streams,"
and his consequent "light and free" feelings that enable him
to catalogue the "luxuries bright" in the landscape about him
(ll. 29ff.).

For a moment now it seems as though the poet has found
the freedom sought by the poem: but perhaps this is only a
freedom from the daemonic presence in the landscape—a
presence that provides a bump on the otherwise smooth
road to Keats's enjoyment of the natural prospect. If this
indeed is the case, then the following descriptions of the
relationships between ancient poets and the myths they con-
ceive are more complicated than we usually grant. Something of this complication, which limits Keats's full commitment to the emotional sphere, may be seen even in those
joyous images of replenishment (a form of repetition) that
nevertheless mask a danger of disappearance:

> If you but scantily hold out the hand,
> That very instant not one will remain—
> But turn your eye, and they are there again.
> [*I Stood Tip-toe,* ll. 78–80]

"They" are only minnows, and there is a natural truth to the
description. In his review of the young poet in the *Examiner,*
however, Leigh Hunt pointed to the relation between fancy

and fact in Keats, to the way Keats "presents us with a fancy,
founded, as all beautiful fancies are, in a strong sense of
what really exists." [1] *I Stood Tip-toe* is strongly fanciful in the
sense that its imagery suggests just this kind of "turn" of the
eye from a confrontation with otherness, and from the spiritual and psychological risk of holding out "the hand" to a
presence that may flee it. In a coincidental image, Yeats
believed it was the subjective poet's lot to hold out hands that
never are satisfied because they never can be satisfied. [2] Keats
in the poem tends to glance away from this antithetical perspective, in the implied hope that a presence not sought will
more readily give of itself—"they are there again." The minnows do return; but landscapes and states of being do so less
readily. The poet's task, if we regard Yeats's statement in the
epigraph to this chapter, may be to sacrifice himself to the
necessary blindness that acknowledges outer loss. To avert
the eye is a means of resisting this antithetical awareness,
which obtrudes upon Keats in *Endymion.*

This sense of the fragility of relationship informs Keats's
presentation of the moon, the muse of the poem that seems
benevolent but eventually is revealed to be potentially a false
mistress—like Keats's later muse-figures, Lamia, Moneta, La
Belle Dame. The moon is the "Maker of sweet poets," not
only because she gilds the world with her light, but because
she is a "Lover of loneliness and wandering, / Of upcast eye
and tender pondering" (ll. 116, 121–22). Traditionally we
cite Wordsworth's description of the mythmaking imagination of the early Greeks as Keat's source for this passage.
In *The Excursion,* which Keats admired exceedingly,
Wordsworth portrays a similar relationship between man's
upcast eye and the tender moon:

> The nightly hunter, lifting a bright eye
> Up towards the crescent moon, with grateful heart
> Called on the lovely wanderer who bestowed
> That timely light, to share his joyous sport;
> And hence, a beaming Goddess with her Nymphs. [3]
>
> [IV, 861–65]

Yet Keats rings significant changes on his source. Wordsworth's mythopoeia is joyous—the hunter invokes the moon with his own power, his "joyous sport." In *I Stood Tiptoe* it is the poet, not the moon, who is the wanderer, and he invokes her power not out of joy but loneliness. She does not then accompany him, as in *The Excursion,* so much as potentially complete him, for his restoring thought is that she is a "lover" of the kind of loneliness he feels.

Is this true in fact, or is it only the poet's fiction? Let us consider, of the several examples of mythopoeia in the poem, the culminating story of the creation of the myth of Endymion (Keats actually called the poem "Endymion" in a letter to Cowden Clarke on December 17, 1816).

> He was a poet, sure a lover too,
> Who stood on Latmos' top, what time there blew
> Soft breezes from the myrtle vale below,
> And brought in faintness solemn, sweet and slow
> A hymn from Dian's temple; while, upswelling,
> The incense went to her own starry dwelling.
> But though her face was clear as infant's eyes,
> Though she stood smiling o'er the sacrifice,
> The poet wept at her so piteous fate,
> Wept that such beauty should be desolate.
> So in fine wrath some golden sounds he won,
> And gave meek Cynthia her Endymion.
>
> [ll. 193–204]

The themes of love, sacrifice, and the poetic imagination, which are interrelated throughout Keats's career—one thinks of the *Ode on a Grecian Urn,* the *Ode to Psyche,* and *The Fall of Hyperion,* among other poems—are brought together here in a manner that anticipates his later development. At first it appears that the benevolence of the poet who stands on Latmos (a middle ground between earth and sky, like Milton's Eden in Collins's *Ode on the Poetical Character*) parallels that of the Greek wanderer in Wordsworth, and more importantly, contradicts the hint at the beginning of the poem that otherness is threatening. But there is a complex "turn" in the passage: "though" the moon "stood smiling" the poet "wept" for her "desolate" fate. That is, he misreads her fate, and his misreading makes possible his completion of her, by means of his gift of Endymion. Thus the mythopoeia is made possible by his interpretive error; but why does he make that error? Why see in a self-sufficient, smiling moon a figure of desolation? Because, it would seem, her self-sufficiency triggers his fear that she does not need him, and he in his loneliness does need her. It is fairly obvious in fact that she is oblivious of his presence. Though earlier in the poem Keats had praised the moon as a lover "Of upcast eye," her face appears to the Latmos poet to be as "clear as infant's eyes," which see without choosing, or shine on all alike—not a sufficient condition for poetic response, we assume.

Do we chase truth too far into the thicket, in Yeats's phrasing, to see in this necessary error a prelude to the character of Keats's own imaginings? His muses share this blindness to externals—and hence obliviousness to him as poet—even though they may seem to include him in their vision. Thus the poet's advice to us in the *Ode on Melancholy* is based on a jarring pun: "feed deep, deep upon her peerless eyes" (l. 20). The mistress's eyes are not only without equal but unseeing, whether the pun is intentional or not, and so may remind us of the eyes of Moneta, which seemed "visionless entire" of "all external things." Whereas Keats's hope in *I Stood Tip-toe* is that the moon is a "Lover" of "upcast eye," by the time he writes *The Fall of Hyperion* he knows better: Moneta's eyes "in blank splendour beamed like the mild moon, / Who comforts those she sees not, who knows not / What eyes are upward cast" (I, 267, 268, 269–71). The contradiction in *I Stood Tip-toe* between latent and manifest content, as it were, is resolved in the later poem, in which the muse's otherness is approached more directly—without that saving turn of the eye.

In 1816, Keats believes the poet is "a lover too," who needs to feel that relationship with the otherness of the moon is possible. The mythopoeia is thus not wholly selfless on his part, for it implies not only his need to love but also his need to be loved. This aspect of the relationship is more clearly seen in the sonnet *Woman! When I Behold Thee Flippant, Vain,* a poem that does not treat mythopoeia but does illuminate the "fine wrath" felt by the Endymion poet:

> But when I see thee meek and kind and tender,
>   Heavens, how desperately do I adore
> Thy winning graces! To be thy defender
>   I hotly burn—to be a Calidore,
> A very Red Cross Knight, a stout Leander,
>   Might I be loved by thee like these of yore.

"Might I be loved": surely this wish is reflected also in the poet's effort to overcome the happy solitude of the moon. Like "vain" women, the moon needs to be made "meek" if it is to become the subject of the poet's love, and though he therefore misreads, he also draws her into human relationship.

"To the ego," Freud says, "living means the same as being loved." [4] Creative life for the poet seems also dependent upon that love, though it is the special love of the muse. Freud's sentence as I quoted it is incomplete, in fact; it continues with an appositive: "—being loved by the super-ego. . . ." The poet's loneliness is a form of division, which can be healed by union with the muse, who has taken on some of the attributes of the super-ego. In the dynamics of this relation we see that poetic wholeness is a form of self-acceptance, and that the outgoingness of song depends upon the intake of the love that provides this—the muse's love and the super-ego's. Freud, we recall, posited division as necessitating the subsequent satisfaction of the ego ideal. The *do ut des* formula Hartman finds at work in the eighteenth-century lyric [5] obtains here as well, though with an additional element: I give (an appreciative perception of your solitude) so that you will give (your love) so that I may give (the myth, in which you may see me in Endymion). In Keats's later poetry, the first term will become, I give of myself: evasions then are minimized.

The complications of the relationship between poet and muse are of importance, not because they demonstrate the poet's possible self-evasions, but because they seem to show that for Keats, even at the outset of his career, the muse's exclusiveness is potentially threatening. Keats's circumambulation forestalls that threat in the same way that Wordsworth's gratulatory belief that Nature never did betray the heart that loved her makes relationship possible for him. Though as critic one hesitates before the threat of Occam's Razor, one cannot help noting that the fair copy version of line 203 ("So in fine wrath some golden sounds be won") reads "So from Apollo's Lyre a tone he won," and one might surmise an Oedipal trespass that adds to the muse's threat. Moreover, the subject of the myth—the young and mortal Endymion winning the comforting divinity of Cynthia—may add to the basis of this surmise. Is the fatheral Apollo being usurped so that the poet can win a motheral Cynthia, and is the goal of the ancient bard's mythopoeia thus regressive? An overview of the poem, however, would place it in the tradition of poems that treat the acquisition of poetic power or identity, and it is in this context that the poet's relations to Cynthia should be approached. Like Collins's Fancy, Cynthia has the power to provide the poet with poetic identity. Identity *is* power, is poetic voice and self-possession. Any violation implied in the relationship of poet to muse has as origin the need for this power. The most important concealed element in the relationship is not sexual but poetic and grows out of need as well as desire: the poet invokes the sublimity of otherness only by reversing its aspect, addressing it as if it needed the poet's tears rather than demanded them.

To bring Cynthia within the sphere of mortal Endymion is a true mingling of gods and men, but that outcome is more declared than won: the sublime is not "meek" and cannot be approached as such. As he develops, Keats takes progressively greater account of the proper dimension of the sublime and of the necessity of poetic self-sacrifice. But for now his concern is restoration, the goal of emotional completion, which is the "humanizing" dimension of poetic creation. The first of two very important results of the marriage of Cynthia and Endymion is the cure of the "languid sick" (l. 223), who awaken from their fevered sleep to discover themselves healed and returned to those they love:

> Young men and maidens at each other gazed
> With hands held back, and motionless, amazed
> To see the brightness in each other's eyes;
> And so they stood, filled with a sweet surprise,
> Until their tongues were loosed in Poesy.
>
> [ll. 231–35]

This is the beautiful myth of restoration that Yeats found in Morris, in which what has been lost is found again, as if wholeness could be achieved by happy returns. It is a primary myth and accordingly has as its object satisfaction in the world and the exclusion of penseroso truths: the model for such satisfaction is the possible return of Eurydice that *L'Allegro* dallies with. The "sweet surprise" that the lovers in Keats experience is a return, much like the surprise that Saturn wishes for in *Hyperion:* "Beautiful things made new, for the surprise / Of the sky-children" (I, 132–33). By the time of the later poem the wish is shown to be impossible, if no less desired. In *I Stood Tip-toe* Keats catches the surprise at the moment it bursts upon the lovers, or rather just as it has "filled" them, as if with love. Each lover is "made new," in Saturn's words, in preparation for a union that is a form of againness, and this surprising renovation enables them to sing. What each lover finds after a dark period is himself once more, a discovery that finds an unexpected reflection in the early appearance, in the poem, of the moon, which progresses toward its own self-realization by "lifting her silver rim / Above a cloud, and with a gradual swim / Coming into the blue with all her light" (ll. 113–15).

The poised moment during which the lovers stand in motionless amazement at their own newness serves to break the continuity of their languid days and so prefigure a rebirth in which they will come into all their light. The plot of this renewal appears also in one of Keats's finest early sonnets, *On First Looking into Chapman's Homer,* written in October 1816, just two months before he completed *I Stood Tip-toe.* In the sonnet the speaker has "Much . . . travelled" before he encounters the renovating voice of Chapman's translation of Homer, which fills him with new wonder and prompts comparisons to earlier discoveries:

> Then felt I like some watcher of the skies
>   When a new planet swims into his ken;
> Or like stout Cortez when with eagle eyes
>   He stared at the Pacific, and all his men
> Looked at each other with a wild surmise—
>   Silent upon a peak in Darien.

Here it is not the moon but a "new" planet that "swims" into the field of vision, silencing all voices of doubt and instilling the wonder of "wild surmise," for what is confronted is a sublime magnitude that augurs expansion of self. The Darien "peak" is therefore not only topographical but emotional—on it we catch Cortez and his men at the moment of their encounter with the sublime and their possible appropriation of it.

In *I Stood Tip-toe* the still moment augurs not only completion but an evasion of death. "Therefore," Keats tells us, "no lover did of anguish die, / But the soft numbers, in that moment spoken, / Made silken ties that never may be broken" (ll. 236–38). Renewal denies the power of death and arrests its progress, which had taken the form of the languid sickness the lovers now have shunned. Love conquers after all; and among the lovers we may number the ancient bards of the poem, as well as Keats as poet. In the high stakes of *I Stood Tip-toe* the poet's own delicate, tip-toed poise awaits this confirmation of the power of poetic imaginings to redeem love.

This significant redemption is effected by a return—that special form of repetition—in which the lovers are reunited and their capacity to love is thus renewed. In this portrayal, Keats has breathed life into the belief that love does not result in death. For the expectation of the passage is that lovers *do* die, despite their loving, and perhaps because love leads to a deathly anguish: loving depletes the self, much as Freud conceived the displacement of libido to objects as the loss of it to the individual. There is an economy that shapes our relationships. What makes it possible for the poet to separate love from death is the strategy of return that allows each lover to "be loved."

It is at this point that Keats's own great outgoingness takes over. The love that has flooded the lovers and given them the strength to love again, leads them to speak "soft numbers" that form unbreakable "silken ties." One sees in this response Keats's own transcendence of the narcissism that is a possible consequence of an emotional inflooding: for Keats's reflex to having achieved a form of poetic centrality or chosenness is always to reciprocate—to establish ties to what is outside the self, much as the mind holds a window open to Love in the later *Ode to Psyche*. It may be that "living means the same as being loved," but for Keats this accurately characterizes only the initial phases of encounters with otherness. What follows is a reflexive outflowing of love that denies the self-involvement of the self that must be loved. Being loved also means loving, to complete the Keatsean paradigm.

Such outflowing almost always tempers poetic ecstasy in Keats and, even in later encounters with the sublime other (who, like the nightingale, would sublime the poet), enables him to maintain his hold on earthly things. This is the basis of the humanizing tendency that is so powerful in the later poetry, though it also may be seen in several early poems. In the sonnet *To my Brother George*, which Keats wrote at Margate in August 1816, Keats recalls himself from the "wonders I this day have seen"—which include witnessing the "bridal night" of Cynthia—to the tie that binds him to George and to primary existence: "But what, without the social thought of thee, / Would be the wonders of the sky and sea?" Social thinking may be on one hand a defense against ecstasy, but it also directs the poet to the poetry of earth and, by necessitating the retention of selfhood, makes it possible for him to draw together otherness and self, the sublime and the emotional. Thus when *I Stood Tip-toe* concludes with the audacious (to Keats) speculation that the marriage of Cynthia and Endymion may have led to the birth of John Keats as poet ("Was there a poet born?"), we recognize that the union of divinity and the mortal Endymion may indeed be seen as poetic birth: the poetry of heaven, already written, gives birth to a poetry of humanized sublimity. Or, since possibility is just newly born, it will. Keats has evaded Collins's fate and found the "delight with liberty" of being the chosen son.

"SLEEP AND POETRY"

In the summer of 1816, several months before he completed *Sleep and Poetry,* Keats composed *Oh, How I Love, on a Fair Summer's Eve,* one of several sonnets he wrote at this time. It is not a major effort—it was not included in *1817*—but its treatment of the relation between emotional and antithetical desires anticipates the important poems that were yet to come. The octet describes a retreat from "All meaner thoughts" and "little cares" that is similar to the flight of poets in the later eighteenth century. But there most of the likeness ends, for Keats projects a successful end to his wish

> to find, with easy quest,
> A fragrant wild with Nature's beauty dressed,
> And there into delight my soul deceive.
> There warm my breast with patriotic love,
> Musing on Milton's fate, on Sidney's bier,
> Till their stern forms before my mind arise—
> Perhaps on the wing of poesy upsoar,
> Full often dropping a delicious tear
> When some melodious sorrow spells mine eyes.

One can see in little in these lines a movement of mind and a corresponding poetic that become a characteristic pattern in Keats's poetry of this period: the poet associates penseroso feelings with the sublimity of Milton and Sidney, and so in the sonnet he not only invokes them but protects his eyes from them. We begin in a pleasance, the trysting place for poets, and the encounter with the sublime takes place only after the poet finds natural delight, as if emotional comfort were necessary to higher confrontations. The approach to sublimity then turns on the fatheral resonance in "patriotic": not that Keats did not genuinely have patriotic feelings, but that the patriots are also his poetic fathers. Yet the presences of Milton and Sidney bring on elegiac feelings, or rather self-elegiac feelings. We hear echoes of the "bier" and "melodious tear" of *Lycidas* (ll. 12, 14) in Keat's mention of Sidney's "bier" and the "delicious tear" and "melodious sorrow" of the speaker himself. The figures of Milton and Sidney rise up as "stern forms" that signify and are identified with a young poet's feelings of "fate"; and the tears that he drops are as much for his being tied to such a destiny as they are for the universality of it. Consequently, though the summons to the sublimity of otherness arises as inevitably as the power of the ego ideal, Keats resists its finality by consigning it to the region of the not-human: to "upsoar" on the "wing of poesy" is to experience the sorrow that "spells"—that is, enchants—the eyes. The poet's eye sees, and sees beyond the "little cares" of ordinary existence, but his enchanted vision is a form of blindness, at least from the perspective of the realm of those cares.

This early expression of Keats's fear for the loss of the sight of common things reappears frequently: in Endymion's ardent wish not to be blinded by Cynthia, in the special blindness of Saturn, and in the poet's inability to see the dark landscape in the *Nightingale* ode, all of which we shall discuss. We may ask at this point what it is that the poet fears to lose sight of, and look to a somewhat later poem for a partial answer. When in the summer of 1818 Keats visited the Burns country, he composed a sonnet in the poet's cottage.

But he thought the poem inadequate to the circumstance, and to compensate wrote a fine poem, the *Lines Written in the Highlands after a Visit to Burns's Country*. Recalling the use of the word in *Oh, How I Love,* Keats reflects on scenes of "patriot battle" and other spots "made known by times of old." He finds a joy deeper even than these in those moments "When weary feet forget themselves" on the route to a special scene—"the castle or the cot where long ago was born / One who was great through mortal days and died of fame unshorn" (ll. 9, 11–12). This forgetfulness of the self, which is repeated in his "forgotten eye [that]is still fast wedded to the ground" (l. 21), may recall the portrait of the goddess Melancholy in *Il Penseroso:* "Thy rapt soul sitting in thine eyes; / There held in holy passion still, / Forget thyself to marble, till / With a sad leaden downward cast / Thou fix them on the earth as fast" (ll. 40–44). Melancholy is self-forgetful in her passion, but Keats least of all wants to forget the self, because he associates selfhood with memory and prefers this to passion, no matter how ecstatic:

> Oh, horrible to lose the sight of well-remembered face,
> Of brother's eyes, of sister's brow, constant to every
>   place,
> Filling the air, as on we move, with portraiture intense,
> More warm than those heroic tints that fill a painter's
>   sense
> When shapes of old come striding by and visages of old,
> Locks shining black, hair scanty grey, and passions
>   manifold.
>
> [ll. 33–38]

This very moving defense of the "portraiture intense" that fills the air around the poet may be read also as a rejection of melancholy ecstasy and the disjuncture necessary to it. Keats has been led to the "spot" that looks out upon the scene of the birth of a poet, and there he chooses continuity and remembrance over discontinuity and the sublime, the "sight" of what is near over the daemonic "shapes of old" that are of another order of vision. Though the specificity is lacking, it seems a reasonable presumption that the tears the poet drops in *Oh, How I Love* are brought on by the threat to the sight of remembered objects that is implicit in poetic up-soaring. The antithetical breaks the "silken ties" that bind the poet to the earthly things he loves; but as poet he must confront the heroic as well as the warm.

Both the flight and the opposed faltering are evident in *Sleep and Poetry* which, in its efforts to define poetry and sketch the poet's place in its story, invites a fuller confronta-tion with the sublime than is usual in *1817*. The comparison suggested in the title is actually a contrast, for Keats wishes us to understand that poetry is "higher beyond thought" even than sleep (l. 19) or "revery" as W. J. Bate defines it.[6] Sleep is "healthful," "secret," "serene," and "More full of visions than a high romance" (ll. 7–10), clearly it does not satisfy the poet. His situation thus parallels that of the speaker of the pseudo-Chaucerian *The Floure and the Leafe* in the passage Keats uses as an epigraph to his poem:

> As I lay in my bed slepe full unmete
> Was unto me, but why that I ne might
> Rest I ne wist, for there n'as erthly wight
> [As I suppose] had more of hertis ese
> Than I, for I n'ad sicknesse nor disese.

The languid sickness that in *I Stood Tip-toe* must be cured by Poesy is notably absent here, and we are left to wonder why Keats is interested in introducing a situation in which sleep is not forthcoming, despite the "hertis ese." Since this—like *I Stood Tip-toe*—is a poem that treats the birth of a poet, it may be just this heart's ease that, in the form of happy anticipation, keeps the poet awake: at the conclusion of the poem he is surprised to learn that his excited thoughts about the future have been intercepted by the first light of dawn. The "hertis ese" may cause sleeplessness in yet an-other way, however, for the expression recalls the "heart-easing" virtue of *L'Allegro*. In this sense, we find Keats imply-ing some dissatisfaction with this emotional category, which is insufficient to bring sleep. The presence of the antithetical sublime tests the strength of Keats's commitment to the heart's ease, and his tendency to portray the sublime but not confront it suggests that his faith in emotional ties needs further confirmation.

From the outset, the "Poesy" we meet in the poem has characteristics of the sublime rather than the emotional: it has a "glory" (and embodies the vanished glory of the dedicatory sonnet); the thought of it is "awful, sweet and holy"; and it tends to chase away "all worldliness and folly" (ll. 24–26). Such chasing is a version of Milton's "Hence," for *Il Penseroso* draws similar associations with worldliness: Philomel sings at night and thus "shunn'st the noise of folly," and the "vain deluding Joys" that are sent hence at the outset of the poem are "The brood of Folly" (ll. 61, 1–2). We thus seem to be departing in *Sleep and Poetry* from the associations of the sublime with the threat of discontinuity that we saw in *Oh, How I Love* and the *Lines* written in Burns's country; but in fact it is the poet's relation to sublimity that the poem tests. The major instance of encounter is foreshadowed by a brief meditation in which the poet suggests an idealization that reflects the magnitude of the sublimity he senses before himself:

> No one who once the glorious sun has seen,
> And all the clouds, and felt his bosom clean
> For his great Maker's presence, but must know
> What 'tis I mean and feel his being glow.
>
> [ll. 41–44]

The sun comprehends Poesy's "glory" in its own, for the "great Maker" in the lines is not only God the Father but also Apollo, who, like Poesy in *I Stood Tip-toe,* is a maker of poets. But the hyperbolic status of sun and clouds drains the poet's own self, though it makes his being "glow" with a correspondent light. This crucial dynamic of purgation and expectation, which leads to the poet's desire to be sacrificed in the following lines, suggests the emptying out of self that inevitably accompanies idealization. To idealize is to grant power to otherness—power over oneself. The *psychological* process of idealization corresponds to the *rhetorical* figure of hyperbole, which rings throughout the poem. Both seem to announce the poet's sacrifice of himself to the glory of otherness; but what they really announce is his quite understandable attempt to assume that glory. Seen from this perspective, idealization and hyperbole serve to counter the poet's sense of the temerity of his trespass, for the assumption of the poetical character, as Collins makes clear, is dependent upon a violation of the sublime other. Collins was excluded from Milton's Eden, but Keats projects a possible acceptance if his sacrifice of self is successful—that is, if he can survive it:

> O Poesy! For thee I grasp my pen
> That am not yet a glorious denizen
> Of thy wide heaven. Yet, to my ardent prayer,
> Yield from thy sanctuary some clear air,
> Smoothed for intoxication by the breath
> Of flowering bays, that I may die a death
> Of luxury and my young spirit follow
> The morning sunbeams to the great Apollo
> Like a fresh sacrifice; *or,* if I can bear
> The o'erwhelming sweets, 'twill bring to me the fair
> Visions of all places.
>
> [ll. 53–63; my emphasis]

When Freud looked back, trying to explain how it all began, this cycle of desire and guilt, he drew upon an anthropological rendering of a primal scene in which a company of brothers murder their primal father: only in this way could they attain what he had, and what they so badly needed—the power that is identity. This explanation is important less for its literal than its allegorical truth, for it dramatizes the guilt that accrues to those who embark upon the inevitable quest for an identity that they associate with another figure. Keats, with his exquisite sensitivity, seems to have known that the power of Milton and other precursors is not won without cost. In what I take as a description of acquisition and its consequence, Keats one week before his twenty-third birthday (October 31, 1818) writes to the George Keatses: "My greatest elevations of soul leave me every time more humbled." [7] The sacrifice Keats envisions in *Sleep and Poetry* is thus a prior atonement for the desire for poetic identity: Keats actually intends less to follow the sunbeams to Apollo than to have visionary power brought "to me." The poet goes beyond the "wild surmise" on the Darien peak and passes into the region of the god, which he hopes is his own region as well.

The god, by implication, is daemonic, for he demands sacrifice in return for vision, as the unconscious must be sacrificed to by the ego. Yet Apollo in actuality is not being won over, for the encounter is only the poet's projection of his own possible future. The deep difficulty of bringing the other into the poet's sphere is the central task of later poems—the great odes and *The Fall of Hyperion*, among others. But in this early poem we sense a resistance on the part of the poet, so that even his quite genuine offer of the self becomes an avoidance of encounter by the alternative proffered by "or." "If" he can bear the "o'erwhelming sweets" he will be granted "fair" visions in which the god's power suffuses a human landscape: "A bowery nook / Will be elysium—an eternal book / Whence I may copy many a lovely saying / About the leaves and flowers, about the playing / Of nymphs in woods and fountains, and the shade / Keeping a silence round a sleeping maid" (ll. 63–68). The god's glory is softened to "lovely" sayings in this statement of the expected consequences of the encounter, and the sayings revitalize the natural world. Keats's hope is that the sublime will be a cure of earth, as it is a cure of disease in *I Stood Tip-toe*. Yet the identification of otherness with a power much like the ego ideal is too apparent for this to be a real possibility. What the poet does, and here we glimpse a central element of his approach, is keep the god at some remove, and so avoid true confrontation, which might obviate the revitalization that is so beneficial to poetic love. It is too simple to designate this a mere avoidance: it reflects a deep-seated feeling on Keats's part that earth is the proper region of poetry and that the god must be brought to this arena if glory and loveliness are to return.

There seems to be, then, an incompatibility between the poet's benevolent identification of Apollo and his true power: the god in fact comes not to liberate but to dominate. Involved in this misidentification is the poet's need for saving discontinuity, but one associated with natural recurrence. We see this in his return to nature, but now a renewed nature, made commensurate with his own desire for relationship. This is both discontinuity and retention, in which the endless succession of moments—Moneta's idea of true time, let us say—is stemmed by a revitalization that makes what had been the past a new present. Keats's evasion of the god is thus liberating, for the god would insist upon an antithetical rejection of repetition—not renewals but opposed realms are the stuff that the gods' dreams are made on. Freud several times in his writings lamented man's inability to give up any source of satisfaction he once enjoyed—hence the past was carried into the present in a less than fortunate way. But Keats's retention (since renewal serves to retain) implies a deeper movement of mind, for retention is an intimation of immortality, an indication that what has been a part of consciousness need not be lost to time.

If there really is a part of the mind that seeks evidences of immortality in the self's ability to retain objects, then the poem suggests it operates as a passive mode, a variety of reading rather than writing. "Life," the poet happily proclaims, is "The reading of an ever-changing tale" (ll. 90, 91). Both reading and change are significant in Keats's description, for it is the series of new moments that make the reading satisfying to the mind. A series of moments without change would take us back to Moneta and pure consciousness. Renewal or repeated newness saves the poet from having to confront the other discontinuity that belongs to the gods; for the time being he can have life brought to him as ever new text, and with the return of loveliness the nymphs are seen again:

A lovely tale of human life we'll read.
And one will teach a tame dove how it best
May fan the cool air gently o'er my rest;
Another, bending o'er her nimble tread,
Will set a green robe floating round her head,
And still will dance with ever varied ease,
Smiling upon the flowers and the trees;
Another will entice me on and on
Through almond blossoms and rich cinnamon,
Till in the bosom of a leafy world
We rest in silence.

[ll. 110–20]

It is remarkable that, though this passage represents a defense against the power of difficult virtue proclaimed by Milton's Attendant Spirit, the goal that Keats seems to desire proves as suspect as Comus's own, and in identical terms: for what is the "rest in silence" but Comus's "timely rest," which points (in Milton) to the presence of death in Comus's wish-fulfillment? Though there is always "Another" nymph to "entice" the poet on in the poem, the end to repetition that each promises is a form of sleep, not poetry.

Writing is of another order. Active and requiring power, it is also antithetical, and Keats recognizes that to achieve it he must pass beyond the "joys" of Flora's realm: "Can I ever bid these joys farewell?" he asks. His immediate reply is "Yes, I must pass them for a nobler life, / Where I may find the agonies, the strife / Of human hearts" (ll. 122–25). Critics have rightly praised the "humanitarian aspect"—the phrase is Walter Jackson Bate's [8]—of this ideal of poetry, but Keats's "Yes" is more problematic than it would seem, or the critics have assumed. Clymene in *Hyperion* laments that "joy is gone" (II, 253), and joy is "ever" bidding adieu in the *Ode on Melancholy* (l. 22). But can the poet so easily bid joy farewell when it comprises his feeling of full relationship—the outer world resanctified for his love? If living means being loved, and perhaps also being loved means loving, what constitutes the nobleness of the strife of "human hearts"? The answers

to these questions must be contained in the portrait of the
visionary charioteer, the active, writing figure whose coming
Keats takes as a sign that he must eventually renounce joy:

> The charioteer with wondrous gesture talks
> To the trees and mountains, and there soon appear
> Shapes of delight, of mystery, and fear,
> Passing along before a dusky space
> Made by some mighty oaks; as they would chase
> Some ever-fleeting music on they sweep.
>
> [ll. 136–41]

The charioteer knows the secret of words and the power of
Orphean invocation: life for him is not the reading of a
lovely tale but the writing of a mysterious one, in a spot
made shady by unaccustomed oaks:

> Most awfully intent,
> The driver of those steeds is forward bent
> And seems to listen. Oh, that I might know
> All that he writes with such a hurrying glow.
>
> [ll. 151–54]

The charioteer's scene is dark and fearful, and though he
writes furiously the poet himself does not know what the
tablets say. Keats resists the message because it must be one
of farewell: the antithetical poet, as Yeats says, is born in
disappointment. Do the "Shapes" the driver sees really por-
tend "delight," or are they only indicative of "mystery" and
"fear"? Is their message one of compensation or disappointment? Keats maintains a distance from the charioteer's
subtler language and from the possibility of assuming his
knowledge. Though the poet cries "Oh, that I might know,"
his not knowing allows further dallying with primary surmise, the delights of Flora that are not easily put by.

The danger of writing is that it is a response to and comprehends difficult knowledge. Yeats, far more antithetical as
a young poet than Keats, nevertheless also wished to preserve a part of himself from the burden of knowing. Looking back in *The Trembling of the Veil* upon his adoption of the

Rose as an early symbol, Yeats recollects that at that time "I prayed to the Red Rose," which to him was a form of "Intellectual Beauty"; and as a further gloss he quotes from his own *To the Rose Upon the Rood of Time:*

> Come near, come near, come near—ah, leave me still
> A little space for the Rose-breath to fill,
> Lest I no more hear common things . . .
> But seek alone to hear the strange things said
> By God to the bright hearts of those long dead,
> And learn to chant a tongue men do not know.[9]

Yeats fears even as he desires the displacement from "common things" that the Rose, as antithetical image, would demand. The "strange things" said by God to those long dead parallel the sounds Keats's charioteer hears from the figures he evokes, and the "tongue" Yeats fears to chant is in the language the driver writes. One wonders at first why Yeats's dead have "bright hearts," and then one realizes that it is so on account of the ultimate sacrifice they have made—they have given up for all time the primary world of Flora and Pan, and so though long dead their vitality remains, as a gift of antithetical wisdom.

When Keats himself (no longer the charioteer) imagines writing it is of a peculiarly limited kind. Earlier in the poem, just after contemplating the visionary rewards of an encounter with Apollo, Keats projects the vocational consequences:

> where I found a spot
> Of awfuller shade, or an enchanted grot,
> Or a green hill o'erspread with chequered dress
> Of flowers and, fearful from its loveliness,
> Write on my tablets all that was permitted,
> All that was for our human senses fitted.
>
> [ll. 75–80]

We are at the scene of rendezvous now, for this is the same "green hill's side" (l. 134) that the charioteer will land upon. Accordingly, it is suffused with the presence of otherness—

the sublime lurks in the shade and in the grot. The poet is made "fearful" of all this (though the "loveliness" presumably is what he seeks), and his fear prevents his entering the scene in any way. Entrance would mean encounter: like the charioteer, Keats as poet would have to address the Shapes or spectres who reside there. But he does not; rather, a certain poetic modesty overtakes his imaginings. "My greatest elevations of soul leave me . . . more humbled." This pervasive fearfulness limits desire, and as a consequence Keats vows to write only what is "permitted," those things that are "for our human senses fitted." In thus curtailing the sublime, Keats is probably following the example set by Wordsworth—his model for adjusting the sublime to human size—who, in the Prospectus to *The Excursion* announces his great theme:

> my voice proclaims
> How exquisitely the individual Mind
> (And the progressive powers perhaps no less
> Of the whole species) to the external World
> Is *fitted:*—and how exquisitely, too—
> Theme this but little heard of among men—
> The external World is *fitted* to the Mind.
>   [ll. 62–68; my emphasis]

Like Wordsworth, Keats fears the power of the sublime to strip the mind naked, to divest it not only of natural things but of all relationship, except that with the daemon of otherness who is, after all, merely another "I." By fitting the sublime to what the senses will accommodate, Keats saves nature for the mind, though at the cost, it is true, of lyrical power. For such diminution enables the poet to continue his survey of descriptive sketches of landscape and poetic history, but it prevents the nakedness of the self that causes the poet to reach out to the dusky region of the daemon. If poetry be considered a fitting as Keats presents it, it will be narrative or descriptive and hard to tell from sleep: we recall the poet later asking in the *Ode to Psyche* whether he sees his

vision with "awakened eyes," and wondering, at the conclusion of the *Nightingale* ode, whether he wakes or sleeps.

What Keats evidently is trying to accomplish is a difficult
reconciliation of the sublime with human limitation, in more
or less Wordsworthian form. It is not that Keats does not
feel the compellingness of the "awfully intent" power of the
charioteer, but that the difficult virtue of the sublime seems
to him so necessarily isolating, at distance from the kind.
This suspicion will make Keats doubt even Wordsworth's
commitment to the "human heart" and will lead to the well-
known denunciation of the older poet's "egotistical sublime."
In *1817* we watch Keats attempting a middle course, following neither the neoclassical ideal of the previous century—
which he believes sacrificed soul to form and so found sleep
rather than Poesy ("Beauty was awake! / Why were ye not
awake?")—nor the egotistical assumption of its power
("strength alone, though of the Muses born, / Is like a fallen
angel"). "Poesy," the poet declares, is "the supreme of
power," is "might half slumbering on its own right arm"
(ll. 236–37). But it cannot be captured by efforts to confine it
or by allowing it free sway, for both of these approaches
forget what Keats calls "the great end / Of Poesy, that it
should be a friend / To soothe the cares and lift the thoughts
of man" (ll. 245–47). Keats chooses relationship rather than
full possession of or complete surrender to Poesy.

The poet will bind otherness to himself as a "friend" then,
as Collins in his ode thinks "Pity" is a "friend to man" (a
phrase Keats echoes in the *Grecian Urn* ode). Keats is moving
toward a dyadic relationship, though by a kind of occluded
vision he construes Poesy as a correspondent to the softer
emotions only—the terror of the sublime is mitigated not by
anything intrinsic to its nature but by the poet's selective
seeing. On this basis the poet can invoke the heart-easing
virtue of *L'Allegro* as a consequence of proper poetic creation: "they shall be accounted poet-kings," he writes, "Who
simply tell the most heart-easing things" (ll. 267–68). To ice
this cake of plenitude he adds as an afterthought, "Oh, may
these joys be ripe before I die"—ripeness as the fruition of

primary, natural growth. One wants not to evaluate this admirable ideal, yet with a prospective sense of Keats's own poetic development we can see that the diminution of the dark power of the sublime tends to produce a monistic poetry that reiterates the emotional satisfaction sought in the eighteenth century but is nevertheless a "partial" song, as Milton says of the music of the fallen angels. The reduction involved here is a gentle fiction of retention, in which a young poet envisions the possible identity of Poesy and heart-easing truths, and as a corollary, the increasing gain that continued devotion will bring. This all is presented to us as an expectation; when the poet internalizes the beneficent muse we will be faced with the psychological sublimation of the *Ode to Psyche*. For now, we rightly doubt that this ideal of poetry can be maintained, or that slumbering "might" is adequate to the experience of loss in gain. Keats already sees that this is a part of the larger dilemma of love, but in *1817* he would like to delay both the necessary egotism of power and the equally necessary sympathy for loss. With *Endymion* we move on to an awesomely ambitious effort to explore that dilemma by a remarkable expansion of the central myth of *I Stood Tiptoe*.

ENDYMION'S "WATCHFUL CARE" (BOOKS I–III)

With his customary generosity, Keats in a letter of March 13, 1818, tried to gloss over his differences with Benjamin Bailey about the value of religious pursuits. "As Tradesmen say every thing is worth what it will fetch," Keats writes his friend, "so probably every mental pursuit takes its reality and worth from the ardour of the pursuer—being in itself a nothing." Having asserted the subjective "reality" of the mind's conceptions, Keats cannot resist an added speculation, that all seemingly external reality may be subdivided into three categories—things "real," things "semireal," and "nothings": "Things real—such as existences of Sun Moon & Stars and passages of Shakspeare—Things semireal such as Love, the Clouds &c which require a greeting of the Spirit to

make them wholly exist—and Nothings which are made
Great and dignified by an ardent pursuit." At this point,
Keats's discourse has become more than an attempt to
soothe the feelings of a close friend reading for holy orders.
The scale running from real things to nothings might also be
read in terms of objectivity and subjectivity, or certainty and
belief. For a young writer who has recently abandoned medical studies for poetry and sees his destiny increasingly as a
difficult relation between power and emotion, these scales
cannot be unimportant. Keats's concern for the worth and
reality of "Nothings"—cyphers from the perspective of physical fact, but necessary presences to the imagination—had
been apparent for the preceding year at least and is met with
throughout *Endymion,* begun the previous April and completed in November, 1817.

In the peripety of *Sleep and Poetry* the departure of the
chariot is followed by the speaker's heightened sense of "real
things" that "would bear along / My soul to nothingness,"
and as a result he is led to question the power of imagination:

> But I will strive
> Against all doubtings and will keep alive
> The thought of that same chariot and the strange
> Journey it went.
>
> [ll. 159–62]

These "doubtings" of the poet's ability to counter the power
of "real things" surface again in *Endymion,* which portrays an
"ardent pursuit" that strives to dignify spiritual truths that to
the voice of doubt (represented by Peona) are merely "Nothings." The famous credo of the poem affirms the permanence of beauty at the same time that it implies doubt: "A
thing of beauty is a joy forever," we begin; but we continue,
"it will never / Pass into nothingness" (ll. 1, 2–3). One is
struck by Keats's insistence upon a concrete "thing" rather
than upon beauty as an intellectual conception. In the Prospectus to *The Excursion,* Wordsworth set out the object of his
own poetic pursuit:

—Beauty—a living Presence of the earth,
  Surpassing the most fair ideal Forms
  Which craft of delicate Spirits hath composed
  From earth's materials—waits upon my steps.

[ll. 42–45]

Wordsworth's "Beauty" characteristically is a mediating image: it seems to ask to be read as metaphor, but there is no tenor for the vehicle—it is a "Presence" that suggests only itself, a numinous quality with no referent to any beyond. But in Keats, as M. A. Goldberg points out, there is a "syntactical subordination" of "beauty" to "thing" that seems to "stress the corporeality of beauty, rather than its abstracted quality." [10] Leaving aside the direction of the subordination, it is clear that Keats wants us to regard beauty in terms of things, not presences; nor is it the "mighty abstract Idea I have of Beauty in all things" of which he writes to the George Keatses on October 24, 1818: that abstracted beauty reflects a further internalization. Rather, Keats's "thing of beauty" reflects his effort to preserve relationship to outer things without recourse to those presences that imply the antithetical. As such, beautiful things "bind us to the earth," as "silken ties" were formed in *I Stood Tip-toe,* though Keats's description of the virtues of these things uncomfortably centers on sleep:

it will never

Pass into nothingness, but still will keep
A bower quiet for us, and a sleep
Full of sweet dreams, and health, and quiet breathing.
Therefore, on every morrow, are we wreathing
A flowery band to bind us to the earth,
Spite of despondence.

[ll. 2–8]

A subtle exercise in belief runs through the passage. According to Henry Stephens, a fellow medical student, the original opening line of the poem read, "A thing of beauty is a constant joy"—that is, an unchanging joy. The first line as we

have it changes constancy to permanence and, by thus keeping beautiful things from "nothingness," keeps us from fear
of death, a dislocation that threatens primary imaginings.
Permanence makes sleep possible (as it was not possible for
the speaker in *The Floure and the Leafe*), and sleep in turn
allows the faith that binds us to earth. The closest parallels to
Keats's triumphant "Therefore" are Wordsworth's bequest
of relationship to Dorothy, "Therefore let the moon / Shine
on thee in thy solitary walk" (*Tintern Abbey,* ll.134–35), and
Coleridge's prayer for Hartley (probably Wordsworth's
model), "Therefore all seasons shall be sweet to thee" (*Frost
at Midnight,* l. 65). All three "Therefores" conclude argu-
ments that make possible the self's willing submission to natural relationship.

Moreover, at the outset of the poem that relationship does
not necessitate exclusion: on the one hand we are bound to
earth, and on the other, crucially, we drink in the heavens in
a sublime ingestion. The sun, the moon, the landscape, "All
lovely tales that we have heard or read," as in *Sleep and
Poetry*—these comprise "An endless fountain of immortal
drink / Pouring unto us from the heaven's brink" (ll. 22–24).
Like Wordsworth in *Tintern Abbey,* Keats connects the landscape with the sublime endlessness of the sky, and the consequent feelings of continuity and of the availability of both
forms of satisfaction enable the poet's progress "Spite of despondence."

This youthful poetic enthusiasm would not need to detain
us except for two considerations: first, the despondence that
Keats hopes to overcome returns forcefully in the fourth
book of the poem; and second, the divided sensibility that
readers have noted in the fourth book partly originates in
Keats's assumption of continuity, which is tested in the initial
contacts between Endymion and Cynthia. Especially since
Glen O. Allen's influential study of the poem,[11] it is impossible to overlook the difficulties Keats faced in concluding it
according to the original myth. The close of the poem seems
to indicate a shift in the goal of Endymion's quest; certainly
the resolution is puzzling—Cynthia, goddess of the moon, is

revealed to be both herself and a girl of the forest. Allen's fine essay has led us to consider a corresponding change in Keats's sensibility: and indeed, the poem was written over a long period of time for a poet who developed so rapidly.

Still, if the complications that inform encounter in the earlier poems are at all prefigurative, we should expect ambivalences almost from the outset. And this I think is the case. When Endymion describes to Peona his first meeting with the unknown creature who turns out to be Cynthia, we discern a division at the core of his existence: "Methought I fainted at the charmèd touch," he begins, "Yet held my recollection" (I, 637–38). The simultaneous presence of swooning and remembrance implies a dual sensibility on Endymion's part. The late Thomas Weiskel, in the most advanced and valuable essay that we have on this poem,[12] sees this division in the following passage:

> Madly did I kiss
> The wooing arms which held me, and did give
> My eyes at once to death—but 'twas to live,
> To take in draughts of life from the gold fount
> Of kind and passionate looks, to count and count
> The moments, by some greedy help that seemed
> A second self, that each might be redeemed
> And plundered of its load of blessedness.
> Ah, desperate mortal!
>
> [I, 653–61]

This first direct encounter with the otherness of Cynthia dramatizes the ambivalence of the sublime. As Endymion enters her embrace he immediately fears a loss of sight, to which he responds by sacrificing his eyes—he gives them "at once to death." We are now at the point in *Sleep and Poetry* when the poet sacrifices self to Apollo. In the early poem the sacrifice is reversed by "or"; here a crucial "but" transforms the outcome, as Endymion learns that the giving of his eyes leads to life, for " 'twas to live." The plot of sacrifice and reward repeats itself, then, but with additional ramifications.

Endymion discovers life not death in the "kind and passionate looks" of his goddess and responds by drinking in
that life, as the opening of the poem promised the accessi-
bility of "An endless fountain of immortal drink." But he
finds he cannot complete this union that calls for his own ecstasy: just at this critical moment, as Weiskel excellently
points out, his ecstasy is halted by the additional presence of
"A second self" that holds his recollection and redeems the
moments. This is indeed the desperation of mortality. But
why does it take this form?

I think we might look to Keats's deeply ambivalent attitude toward otherness for part of the explanation. Readers
of *Sleep and Poetry* cannot help but notice that there is a ma-
levolent aspect to the sublime, but that at the same time
there is no renovation of the poet's landscape without its
presence. The sense of "real things" that descends upon the
poet in the wake of the charioteer comes "doubly strong"
(l. 157) because those things are intrinsically killing to the
imagination, and especially so without the presence of the
driver and his promise of ascent. The poet cannot give up
the desire to retain his ties to those around him, the portraiture intense that has a more sober coloring than the heroic
scenes of earlier times. Keats in just a few months, as we
shall see, will write that Milton had committed "himself to
the Extreme," where commitment implies belief and the Extreme is the otherness that is Milton's godly sublime. But
Keats, who feels so exquisitely the claims of earth, cannot so
commit himself, and because he cannot, a "greedy self" rises
to assure him of future remembrance. I am suggesting, in
other words, that the redemption of time will result from the
preservation of it in memory, and the ability to go *back* to it
is made necessary by Endymion's sense that he cannot submit to the sublime. The greedy self recalls the "greediest
eye" of *I Stood Tip-toe*, which needed the reassurance of natural plenitude when faced with the gentle shock of a spectral
landscape. The economy of relationship still holds true,
however much Endymion would like to be sublimed. The
poet's overriding sense seems to be that full commitment is

impossible without belief, and retention is the necessary if melancholy consequence.

Is this a failure of love or its proper Keatsean definition, one wonders. After all, if "life" is a part of Cynthia's realm, why should resistance to it be so powerful? The basic opposition, it seems clear, is between the other whose power is antithetical life and the second self that is a form of self-possession. The poet's dilemma is that without a commitment to the extreme that is power, he cannot have a complete relationship with otherness (only with natural objects)—yet he has conferred the means of his own self-acceptance upon Cynthia, whose kind and passionate looks are necessary to his living. What is being described on one level in the passage is the failure of Endymion's love, for the rising of the second self is equivalent to the origination of doubt. Endymion cannot commit himself to Cynthia because he *believes* he is divorced from her, though because so much of his happiness seems to lie with her, he cannot easily recognize his separation. This belief, which I think is fundamental to Keats's invocations of the sublime, destines otherness to be construed as separate from the self, and as a consequence, even the seeming satisfaction of embrace is touched by fear and doubt.

There is a more essential way in which Keats's belief in the separation of the sublime colors his sense of a divine otherness. In a beautiful meditation on relationship, Shelley in his essay *On Love* surmised that tears and not joyous laughter attend the realization of one's deepest wishes. "In the motion of the very leaves of spring," Shelley writes, "in the blue air, there is then found a secret correspondence with our heart. There is eloquence in the tongueless wind, and a melody in the flowing brooks and the rustling of the reeds beside them, which by their inconceivable relation to something within the soul, awaken the spirits to a dance of breathless rapture, and bring tears of mysterious tenderness to the eyes, like . . . the voice of one beloved singing to you alone." [13] Why should tears be the response to discovery of the voice of the "beloved"? The dynamic largely evades intellection, as Shel-

ley implies, though a crude analysis might yield the broad
suggestion that the lover did not expect to find a secret correspondent, because his deepest self-belief told him he was
alone. The voice of the beloved—that is, the awakening of
the spirits to relationship—therefore comes as a surprise,
because his attitude toward outer things has been deter-
mined by his feelings of abandonment or forlornness. Poetic
quests for the sublime are predicated on a Shelleyan "secret
correspondence," but the hope for its discovery is dependent
upon a belief of the kind we see in Keats.

The feeling of being forlorn is one dimension of fallenness, and readers seem to agree with Glen Allen that Endymion (unlike his fellow Latmians) is fallen when we meet
him. Lear, in the play that Keats loved (and that echoes
through the later books of the poem), bursts into tears upon
being reunited with Cordelia not only because her return is
so unexpected, but also because he feels strongly the burden
of his own error: "Thou art a soul in bliss," he begins, "but I
am bound / Upon a wheel of fire" (IV, vii, 46–47). "But I":
the sense of fall is one of separation, even at the moment of
return. One does not want to obscure Shelley's description
by piling examples around it, but if we do not see the nature
of Endymion's ambivalence, we will force ourselves into the
circular explanations of allegory.

Perhaps now we can add some further shading to our earlier sketch of poetic relationship in Keats. "Self-surrender,"
as Yeats calls it, to Keats means laying to rest the "greedy,"
"second self" that intrudes upon encounters with a sublime
otherness and inhibits the poet's ecstasy or being sublimed.
Keats in the induction to *Endymion* sets forth a belief in the
"essences" of a natural relationship. His faith is that life re-
sides in the bound existence of this second self, rather than
in the sublime:

> Nor do we merely feel these essences
> For one short hour; no, even as the trees
> That whisper round a temple become soon
> Dear as the temple's self, so does the moon,

> The passion poesy, glories infinite,
> Haunt us till they become a cheering light
> Unto our souls, and bound to us so fast
> That, whether there be shine or gloom o'ercast,
> They always must be with us, or we die.
>
> [I, 25–33]

To give up these objects, as contact with Cynthia necessitates, is to experience the object-loss that is a form of death—"we die." Yet paradoxically, as we have seen, Endymion finds that Cynthia brings him "life." Life to one aspect of the hero is death to another: the desire for outer relationship conflicts with the desire for the love that brings self-acceptance, though the poet needs both. To recognize this need and its duality is to begin to move toward the partial resolution of oxymoron, the meeting place on Yeats's cross. The strained ending of *Endymion* results from a lack of such a recognition when Keats began the poem: duality lives in book four as a double (or divided) identity.

The portion of the self that will not be enchanted seeks self-possession or self-consciousness, an awareness of the self. The sublime experience with Cynthia is much like a moment of vision, in other Romantic poems and in Keats's own poetry, but with this crucial difference: vision is usually dependent upon a putting to sleep of the second self, the sense of identity:

> that serene and blessed mood,
> In which the affections gently lead us on,—
> Until, the breath of this corporeal frame
> And even the motion of our human blood
> Almost suspended, we are laid asleep
> In body, and become a living soul.

These lines (41–46) from Wordsworth's *Tintern Abbey* suggest the dual nature of the sleep and wakefulness of vision. In Wordsworth the resistant element is quite literally a body ego, a self that knows itself through physical existence. Subduing this consciousness so that the "soul" might live parallels Endymion's discovery that his submission to death has brought him life. The same admixture of ingredients can be found in Yeats:

> The purpose of rhythm . . . is to prolong the moment of contemplation, the moment when we are both asleep and awake . . . by hushing us with an alluring monotony, while it holds us waking by variety, to keep us in that state of perhaps real trance, in which the mind liberated from the pressure of the will is unfolded in symbols.[14]

Will, body, second self: all are varieties of the selfhood that perplexes and retards the poet's effort to lose himself to vision. Keats is unique in retaining a consciousness that will not be put by, as in the earlier poetry the poet feared that vision might end "social" relationship. The desire for visionary freedom necessarily involves the power of enchantment. To take on Cynthia's power Endymion must open himself out to her by submitting to her power—such submission being a gesture of love. The episode begins with his so doing but quickly proceeds to the reflexive counting of moments, an indication that self-consciousness is present and that Endymion in effect has qualified his receptiveness to Cynthia. A fear of not returning, a form of separation, lurks in the passage, as the Knight of the later poem *La Belle Dame Sans Merci* fears that he is imprisoned "in thrall" as well as enthralled. Captivated.

Paul de Man observes that "Modernity exists in the form of a desire to wipe out whatever came earlier in the hope of reaching at last a point that could be called a true present, a point of origin that marks a new departure."[15] If we think of de Man's insight in terms of vision, we might say that the poet wishes to anesthetize his tendency to recollect so that vision can provide him with a departure from the sense of continuity with a present that is always becoming a past—the present, de Man says, is "a passing experience." To escape his involvement in this process, the poet seeks a freedom from the past that is the freedom of discontinuity, in which he chooses to give himself to the moment, in the hope that it is a true present. This is the temptation of nowness. Yeats describes this immersion as a Faustian attempt to separate the moment from its progress, and hold it:

> We are taken into a clear light and are forgetful even of our own names and actions and yet in perfect possession of ourselves murmur like Faust, 'Stay moment,' and murmur in vain.[16]

The "life" that Endymion finds in his contact with Cynthia, Yeats sees as a perfect and complete "possession" of the self—but this is the *authentic* self, Wordsworth's "living soul." All else is forgotten or put to sleep in the moment, and the poet thereby escapes the burden of continuity. Seemingly a preserver of vision, but actually opposed to it, Endymion's second self "counts and counts" the moments in an effort to redeem them that masks a fear that they are merely passing, that there is no authentic present: the Faustian moment gives way to successiveness.

Though I have ascribed a good portion of the "second self" to a failure of belief, the poem suggests that there is also a positive dimension to it. As late as the middle of the fourth book, Endymion still has not overcome his need for recollection, but his reasons for its presence are formidable. "Say, beautifullest," he addresses his elusive lover, "shall I never think?"

> Oh, thou could'st foster me beyond the brink
> Of recollection, make my watchful care
> Close up its bloodshot eyes, nor see despair!
>   [IV, 305–08]

Endymion opposes a "watchful care" to what Keats earlier called the "poet's eye." To Endymion then, in this *primary* mood, vision is a sleep rather than an awakening, for it fails to comprehend the moral and ethical necessities of witnessing human suffering. Primary seeing maintains an awareness of despair that accrues from memory. (The association between sight and memory is not uncommon in Keats: in the

second ode to Fanny Brawne the poet asks, "What can I do
to drive away / Remembrance from my eyes?") Keats probably is basing his claims for primary existence on the resolution of Wordsworth's *Intimations* ode, which finds consolation
in "an eye / That hath kept watch o'er man's mortality"
(ll. 198–99). Endymion's "watchful care" is less a resolution or
synthesis than an alternative choice—social memory rather
than blind rapture—that *emotionalizes* experience. This is
Yeats's "gentle self-surrender" rather than his surrender to
the daemon, where "gentle" connotes the sublimated pleasure of emotional attachment. It is of the greatest importance, I think, to see that Keats is not opposing imaginative
escapism to real human pain, but a personal daemon to the
landscape of attachment, which fills the memory as with
thoughts of love—even though despair is so pervasive.

Endymion therefore cannot accept Cynthia fully without
softening her identity by bathing her in the somewhat narcist waters of the emotions. At the same time, the text
suggests that she is what Shelley in the essay *On Love* calls a
proper "antitype": she is the "completed form of all completeness" (I, 606) and so can complete Endymion, whose
fall is a form of division. The Latmians imply Cynthia's antithetical identity in their prayers for natural completion—
Pan, they believe, informs "the fresh budding year / And all
its completions" (I, 259–60)—but Endymion nevertheless
stoutly defends the virtue of "essence" to the dubious Peona.
Endymion is motivated to seek a "fellowship" with an essence like Cynthia's despite Peona's warning that essence
and sleep are indistinguishable. "How light / Must dreams
themselves be," she urges him to believe, "seeing they're
more slight / Than the mere nothing that engenders them"
(I, 754–56). Like the poet before Moneta in *The Fall of Hyperion,* Endymion must argue the separateness of imagination and dream and, correspondingly, the object of his love
and any mere "slumberous phantasm" (I, 771).

> Wherein lies happiness? In that which becks
> Our ready minds to fellowship divine,

> A fellowship with essence, till we shine
> Full alchemized, and free of space.
>
> [I, 777–80]

Semantically, "fellowship" is congruent with the combined self-surrender and self-possession that one finds at the heart of the complete visionary experience. As such the term anticipates Keats's remarkable description of the state of poetic creativity he calls—in a letter in late December, 1817, to his brothers—*"Negative Capability,"* the ability to fully conjure the mystery of existence by remaining passive and suspended, even in doubt, rather than imposing false reasoning on experience. But in practice Endymion cannot become "Full alchemized," because he cannot surrender self entirely to otherness—the idea is compelling but not emotionally fulfilling.

Or we might say that Endymion wants to be taken, as if by alchemization, and wants to diminish his selfhood but does not have the requisite faith in Cynthia. He sets his goal as a state of "oneness" that is equivalent to Yeats's Unity of Being and seeks the "Richer entanglements" and "enthralments" that are "self-destroying," in which self can be trammeled up. Of all these, the "chief intensity" is love:

> at the tip-top
> There hangs by unseen film an orbèd drop
> Of light, and that is love. Its influence,
> Thrown in our eyes, genders a novel sense,
> At which we start and fret, till in the end,
> Melting into its radiance, we blend,
> Mingle, and so become a part of it—
> Nor with aught else can our souls interknit
> So wingedly. When we combine therewith,
> Life's self is nourished.
>
> [I, 805–14]

This passage, which is seemingly straightforward, is extremely problematic, for the "love" that throws its "influence" in our *eyes* threatens a blindness similar to that which

Endymion fears in giving his eyes to death and Cynthia. The
influence even of love seems to him to be a form of loss: we
"start and fret" when confronted with it, until at last we submit. We submit, but a spectral presence evokes the fear that
our eyes will lose the world, that union with essence requires
renunciation. This is a fear that Yeats, among other poets,
shares. The question in the epigraph to this chapter echoes
in this surmise on the origin of the identification between
blindness and poetry: "In primitive times the blind man became a poet," Yeats speculates, "because he had to be driven
out of activities all his nature cried for. . . ." [17] Freud's in-
terpretation of blindness as the equivalent of castration may
not be wholly irrelevant to Endymion's erotic quest, but as
poet Keats is concerned with another trespass: the violence
done to the self by the poet's yielding to the temptation of
sublimity. The self that is "Life's self" may be nourished by a
union with essence, but the union is described in terms of a
giving over, as one melts into *its* radiance and becomes a part
of *it*. Yet it appears that the sublimed self is the authentic
self of the poet, or at any rate the antithetical poet, and the
fear of the "influence, / Thrown in our eyes" by the "orbèd
drop / Of light" may be in part a fear of the poet who most
haunts Keats's poetry, who in his blindness lamented the loss
of light to his own eyes, "So thick a drop serene hath
quencht their Orbs"; but whose fatheral presence gives to
spectral shadings their ghostly power.

There is then an ambivalence at the core of Keats's attitude toward those "enthralments far / More self-destroying"
as toward love in general. The love that threatens our sight
is our sense of the other's love *of us,* and the poet who would
evade at least a portion of its antithetical summons must
evade it as well. Keats seems to have sensed this almost from
the beginning of his career, and perhaps the necessity of
maintaining a hold on primary feelings (which inform the
poetry of earth) helps to account for his rhetorical sidestep-
ping of the early sublime personages. Freud surmised that
the dead gods become daemons of the mind—the other we
loved earlier returns as a present spectre. I do not think we

have appreciated fully the extent to which Keats thought of
poetry as an expression of love, and how much the dialectic
of a love relationship informs encounters in the poems.
Keats describes his poetic task as treading "The path of love
and poesy" and sees his goal as uprearing "Love's standard
on the battlements of song" (II, 38, 41)—that is, transforming the heroic epic to the truer poetry of love. That is his
goal, yet readers have agreed that it remains unrealized in
the poem.

Some of the difficulty seems to arise from a discrepancy
between the poet's *sense* of the muse—his fear for his eyesight, his regret for her distance from earth—and his unwill-
ingness to acknowledge her daemonic aspect. Yeats came to
believe that during the course of a poet's development the
world grew smaller in his eyes, but that which remained
greater than himself necessarily filled him with sorrow. But,
Yeats warns, "there is submission in a pure sorrow," and so
"we should sorrow alone over what is greater than ourselves,
nor too soon admit that greatness. . . ." [18] Keats, I think, is
unwilling to see sorrow in the solitary completeness of the
muse, as Endymion is reluctant to "submit" to Cynthia. Why
the greatness of the muse should inevitably be the cause of
sorrow is not clear, even if we turn to Freud, whose explanation of the transformation of gods to daemons is really only
descriptive. In his essay on *The 'Uncanny,'* Freud suggests
that men create doubles of themselves out of a feeling of
"unbounded self-love," but that as soon as this narcist stage
is "surmounted," the double "reverses its aspect. From having been an assurance of immortality, it becomes the uncanny harbinger of death." [19] By reading these sentences
together with *On Narcissism* and *The Ego and the Id,* we can
see that the self surmounts narcissism at the same time that
it forms an ego ideal. Ambivalence and the daemonic arise
simultaneously, though the process still wants explanation.

Keats's later poems indicate his increasing recognition of
the muse's power to destroy as well as redeem, and the dialectic of love grows to include the poet's necessary submission as a prelude to dialogue. Before turning to the clear

beginning of this in book four of *Endymion,* however, let us
glance at the fascinating figure of Glaucus, who is the poet
who loved incorrectly and so failed to enter relationship. As
such, by the way, he anticipates the later portrait of the
frozen Saturn in *Hyperion,* as Endymion himself grows into
Apollo.[20] Glaucus's personal history begins in "silent happiness" and "slumberous ease" (III, 324), as he tells Endymion.
He thus risks both the silence and sleep that Endymion also
must overcome. But Glaucus errs in choosing the "tempting
fruit" of a "dalliance supreme"—a "long love-dream" (III,
442, 439, 440). Like Spenser's Fradubio, Glaucus leaves his
true love behind and chooses the dangerous though completely sensual love of Circe and, as a consequence, needs
the help of Endymion to escape her spell.

Though Endymion is thus necessary to Glaucus's release,
it is also the case that Glaucus's story is meant to warn him
against making a similarly improper choice in love. For
Glaucus—the fisherman who cast his "nets" over the water
while "Keeping in wait whole days for Neptune's voice" (III,
367, 355)—is the figure of the poet who failed to conjure
that voice and so fell into silence. Glaucus sought the "freedom" from Neptune's kingdom (III, 391) that is the sublime,
but he achieves instead only irony. He himself describes this
as a change from "specious heaven" to "real hell" (III, 476):
the sublime would have raised him to real heaven. This transition reveals itself rhetorically in ironic repetitions: instead
of mastering the sublime with his own nets he is caught in
Circe's net (III, 427); instead of the "Shapes unseen" that,
before his meeting with Circe, flash temptingly in the waters
he fishes, he is presented with the wretched "shapes, wizard
and brute" that surround his dark goddess (III, 343, 500);
and so on. Sensuality for Glaucus therefore becomes not the
endless repetition of identical experience but a repetition
that continually re-enacts his own fall and reminds Endymion of the risk in seeking a more than mortal love, or in
choosing the freedom of essence.

Endymion, for his part, understands that Cynthia's region
is dangerous but believes that her love for him keeps him

safe. During his first encounter with her he describes what he takes to be her beneficence: "Felt too, I was not fearful, nor alone, / But lapped and lulled along the dangerous sky" (I, 645–46). Comus's mother, the same Circe who deceived Glaucus, would take the prisoned soul and "lap" it in Elysium. The real danger that Endymion faced at the outset of his quest was to believe that the sky could be lapped for him, that the sublime, like Milton's raven down of darkness, could be smoothed until it smiled. Glaucus's story of Circe is meant to dispel that false expectation and prepare Endymion for the Indian Maiden and her awareness of human sorrow in book four, to which we now turn.

3

The Voice of Poetic Love

> nor could the Muse defend
> Her Son.
>
> Milton, *Paradise Lost,* VII

A New Voice: "Endymion," Book Four

A further dilemma at the center of the Romantic experience of the sublime is not only that sublimity is tied to otherness, and the poet must yield selfhood in order to appropriate power to himself; but that though the fatheral or parental otherness requires the poet's renunciation if he is to assume poetic identity, the young poet *needs* the power of the other in order to renounce. Renunciation seems to be a prerequisite to internalization; but in fact there can be no renunciation without the assumption of a power that is more than one's own, for what is being renounced is the world of instinctual desire, of natural and emotional (in Yeats's sense) being. If we recall Freud now, we see that this almost exactly parallels his explanation of the breaking of the Oedipal complex and the birth of the super-ego: according to Freud, the power of the father is assumed in order to repress forbidden desires—though for the poet these are broadly instinctual. As a second but no less important consequence, the power that is internalized becomes a power over the self, much as fatheral figures become ego ideals. Dilemmas seem to lead easily to misfortunes. The difference between seeking or invoking the power of otherness and learning that one has granted power to it, which I take as a difference between young poets and more mature ones, may be seen in the following description, which seems arbitrary but which I think characterizes one aspect of Keats's own development: the young poet, as in *Sleep and Poetry,* believes he must sacrifice self in order to win favor from the muse; the mature poet, as in the *Ode on a Grecian Urn,* believes he is *being* sacrificed as a result of the muse's dark power. This transition begins in the fourth book of *Endymion.*

Endymion portrays several attempts at "freedom": Endymion's quest for freedom from the natural world of the Latmians; Glaucus's quest to escape the repetition of days spent in Neptune's world; and the poet's or speaker's own desire for deliverance from physical restriction, voiced in the proem to book four. Figuratively, each type of natural restraint is associated with seeing. When Endymion, for example, fears the coming of Cynthia and the loss of his natural happiness he cries out, "Oh, be kind, / Keep back thine influence, and do not blind / My sovereign vision" (III, 181–83). This fear for literal vision, together with other instances we have considered, is also a fear for the self that is dependent upon memory, since as we have seen eyesight and remembrance are associated in Keats. If the dilemma I have pointed to is relevant, it is just this form of seeing and remembering that Endymion will have to renounce, and he will have to call upon Cynthia to help him do so.

The poem is not quite so simply organized, however. Its resolution does turn upon Endymion's transcendence of merely physical seeing, but the ending is complicated by what appears to be a change in sensibility that Keats himself was undergoing. We shall discuss this change in its place; for now, let us briefly consider the mode of transcendence or partial transcendence of sight. In the fourth book of *Endymion* this takes the form of a substitution of voice and hearing for eyes and sight—an alternative sense for an alternative existence. We see this foreshadowed in Glaucus's unsuccessful waiting "whole days for Neptune's voice" and in a similar poised moment that attends a meeting between Endymion and Cynthia in book two:

And, but from the deep cavern there was borne
A voice, he had been froze to senseless stone.
[II, 199–200]

The voice that rises from the cavern to save the natural man
is the voice of the other, heard in the calm of thought or in
the trances of the blast, or in the Keatsean moment of
breathless anticipation. It augurs a future that breaks with
the past, a moment of origin that is authentically revitalizing;
and always, even in Wordsworth, it lies beneath the reality
that is seen:

For I have learned
To look on nature, not as in the hour
Of thoughtless youth; but hearing oftentimes
The still, sad music of humanity.
[*Tintern Abbey,* ll. 88–91]

The voice Endymion overhears belongs to the Indian
Maiden he unexpectedly comes upon in the forest. The
Maiden, whose portrait seems greatly indebted to the Cash-
mir maid in Shelley's *Alastor,* represents an earthly alternative to the divinity of the moon and to the goddess with
whom Endymion has fallen in love. Both the goddess and
the Indian are Cynthia in disguise, of course, but Endymion
must decide without knowing this, as if he were choosing
among metal caskets. Moreover, the Indian speaks for a different kind of love, it would seem, from that of the gods.
She is full of "tenderness" (IV, 61) rather than the power to
blind, and the love she dreams of is based upon return, in
which a lost partner is granted a freedom that recalls the
freedom sought by the questers in the poem and by Orpheus for Eurydice in *L'Allegro:* "Oh, for Hermes' wand,"
the Indian Maiden muses,

To touch this flower into human shape!
That woodland Hyacinthus could escape
From his green prison.
[IV, 66–69]

Her request has deep resonances, for Glaucus too had been imprisoned, and in the invocation to the fourth book the poet complains of the "prison" of the body (III, 296; IV, 20). Both Glaucus and the narrator, however, think to escape prison by choosing the sublime: Glaucus plunges into the underwater world of Neptune, and the narrator longs for a spirit's wings. Though she has known sorrow, the Maiden seeks to metamorphose the god into "human shape"— freedom for her is the same as human existence. This is so because she can love, unlike Endymion, who as a self-proclaimed "lord / Of flowers" (IV, 937–38) needs to learn the submission of which she is capable:

> My soul doth melt
> For the unhappy youth. Love! I have felt
> So faint a kindness, such a meek surrender
> To what my own full thoughts had made too tender,
> That but for tears my life had fled away!
>
> [IV, 71–75]

Where Endymion failed to surrender self to Cynthia, she surrenders fully, though inspired only by her own thoughts, and though she seeks no wonder but the human face, as Moneta later will advise the poet. The Maiden has passed the brink of recollection and is held back or contained within self only by her "tears"—tears of tenderness, and perhaps too a lament for the loss of self that love demands. She realizes the depth of sympathy or empathy that Keats himself displays throughout his letters and in much of his poetry. Her emotional yielding is an "enthralment" that is "self-destroying," and elicits from her a remarkable praise of the "voice of love," the music that enthralls. "Ye deaf and sense-less minutes of the day," she begins, castigating merely successive time,

> And thou, old forest, hold ye this for true,
> There is no lightning, no authentic dew
> But in the eye of love. There's not a sound,
> Melodious howsoever, can confound

The heavens and earth in one to such a death
As doth the voice of love.

[IV, 76–82]

In this extraordinary proclamation the Maiden does nothing less than transform the traditional relationship of voice
and sublimity. When the Lady sings in *Comus* the Attendant
Spirit associates her song with the music of the spheres and
takes in "strains that might create a soul / Under the ribs of
Death." Her song brings him heaven, much as the speaker of
Il Penseroso sought the ecstasy that would bring "all heaven"
before his eyes. The Maiden humanizes this divine otherness: her "voice of love" brings one not heaven but a state in
which internal heaven and earth are confused and put to
rest. She suggests, therefore, that otherness destroys the self
but redeems by coming as love; and because love includes
sorrow it renders the understanding that is forgiveness, and
so one can submit to its power with gain as well as loss.

The Indian Maiden goes on to sing her song "O Sorrow,"
the sorrow of love. At this point the music of spring is about
to become the music of autumn, and we have the possibility
of an authentic humanized sublime. Endymion does not follow along, however, even though he impetuously tells the
Maiden that her tears "have given me a thirst / To meet
oblivion" (IV, 123–24). Our hero, it seems, is still a man of
divided soul, who would like both the Cynthia of heaven and
the Indian of earth. When the Maiden finishes her song he
tries hard to commit himself to her, but his words suggest
his dilemma: "Do gently murder half my soul," he tells her,
"and I / Shall feel the other half so utterly" (IV, 309–10).

If the Indian corresponds to only half of the ideal of
beauty that Endymion pursues, Cynthia in her identity as
goddess also is only half fulfilling. After one of his visionary
sleeps, Endymion rises to find that his dream of the goddess
has been realized: he "Beheld awake his very dream," we are
told (IV, 436). This should be a crucial moment for Endymion, for in his important letter of November 22, 1817, to
Bailey, Keats draws his well-known parallel between the

imagination and the dream Adam has of Eve's creation, during which he slept, but "Fancy," his "internal sight," remained awake in mute witness to reality (*Paradise Lost*, VIII, 452–90): "The Imagination may be compared to Adam's dream," Keats writes, "—he awoke and found it truth." [1] Endymion similarly awakens to truth and, as he does so, would appear to dispel even Peona's grave doubts of the utility of dreaming. But just as Lycius encounters distractions when he finally is wed to Lamia, Endymion cannot seize his new reality. Instead he discovers he is in a "state perplexing," finds himself not full of voice but "tongue-tied," and as he advances toward her he is halted: "Ah, what perplexity," Keats repeats (IV, 439, 444, 447).

A distance appears here between the narrator and Endymion. Keats had begun the poem with the feeling that for him Endymion was one of those "essences" that become a cheering light: "Therefore, 'tis with full happiness that I / Will trace the story of Endymion. / The very music of the name has gone / Into my being," he proclaimed confidently (I, 34–37). But the yearning after the beautiful, of which Keats was so fond of writing—in his letter of October 14–31, 1818, to the George Keatses, for example, he says he should be "enviably" happy with his "Passion" for "the beautiful"—has come to confusion in Endymion, who cannot relate Cynthia to the Maiden. Hence the irony of Keats's repetition of "perplexity," a word that appears with similar significance in a later description of Lamia, who as a goddess (of sorts) can "unperplex bliss from its neighbor pain" (I, 192). As the later poem makes clear, such unperplexing works for gods, not men. Endymion's perplexity is at odds with the myth of the poem, which calls for him to be united with Cynthia in her divine identity. And the term parodies the proper stance of the poet-quester, who mingles contraries rather than is confused by them.

This I think is an important moment in the poem for Keats himself, whose own quest until now has not differed significantly from Endymion's. Endymion cannot choose between what he sees as exclusive identities, one incorporating freedom, the other, duality. Keats as poet is moving swiftly toward the latter, though as poet of a poem called *Endymion,* he must have his hero end with Cynthia. Put another way, the Indian Maiden recalls the ambivalence of Endymion's own past, the sorrow that, though unnoticed, prompted his search for freedom from earthly confines. She, in effect, returns him to his "watchful care," for her definition of love cannot be abstracted from sorrow. As goddess, however, Cynthia promises a break from the human past and the joy of thus mastering it. Keats could not help but feel the attractiveness of that promise, that joyous un-self-consciousness that as poet he seeks and yet resists.

When Endymion accepts (even partly) sorrow as a standard of love, he begins to accept also his own division and begins the representation of the mature poet's feeling of being sacrificed. This is not to say that at some level the feeling was not there all the time, or that Endymion was not fallen when we met him in book one. It is to say that acceptance of his situation begins here: we end the dominance of the strong tendency in Keats's early poems to turn the eye from possible loss, in the hope of beneficent returns. I do not think there can be any meaningful relation to otherness without this acknowledgment of the self's own lack of power; though as I have suggested, this does not complete the relationship. But it is a crucial beginning. Endymion's love for the Indian Maiden, who appears to him to be broken by love yet still loving, implies an acceptance of the diminished self and presages Keats's own strong feelings concerning the necessity of human suffering in an earthly existence that is more a vale of soul-making than a vale of tears, as a later letter has it.

I suggest also that in this attachment to sorrow there are the beginnings of a self-acceptance that I find missing in the earlier poetry, however idealized the portrayals of human love there. The quite genuine desire for the repression that is the sublime calls forth or rather expresses a subtle but insidious form of self-hatred: to desire the repressive power of otherness *over* the self is to turn against the self. So Yeats understood his own great desire for the antithetical, though his insight came only after that period of his life had passed. The pursuit of a beauty that is "absolute and external," Yeats writes in 1932, "requires, to strike a balance, hatred as absolute." [2] We will discuss Yeats's complex relation to antithetical beauty in the last chapter, but this poet who was so concerned with self-acceptance and self-forgiveness surely intended us to understand "hatred" as a feeling for the self as well as for the natural things that keep us from that absolute beauty—the beauty of Cynthia in her proper identity as goddess. Even a tentative aggrandizement of sorrow represents an attempt to love the self that is broken, despite its division.

This argument, carried to its limits, would identify the Indian Maiden with self-acceptance and Cynthia with self-repression: but this cannot be the whole story, or what incentive would there be for Endymion to have begun by seeking Cynthia? Initial narcissism, Freud says, is broken by two radical departures, the formation of relationships and the rise of an ego ideal. Later self-hatred, which to his dismay Freud found increases with time, results from the ego ideal's rejection of the ego, which I take as a parallel to the muse's possible rejection of the poet, in an outward version of the inner struggle. The poet's acceptance of his own brokenness, his own sorrow, defuses, as it were, the threat of the muse—he has already acknowledged the brokenness *that she partly has caused.* This last point may seem a radical addition to our paradigm, but it is entirely consistent with both Freud and the narrative of *Endymion.* Endymion's "fall" begins his quest for Cynthia, the muse who he hopes will heal the rift he experiences. In Keats's early poems, as we have seen, there is a tendency to deny the potential threat of otherness: thus, for example, the moon in *I Stood Tip-toe* seems to know what eyes are upward cast, as Moneta, the muse in actuality, does not. But the muse does not come to love—she must be made to do so. The love of sorrow is a power *over* her otherness, an affirmation of self in the face of her strict denials, and makes possible a true meeting with the necessary power that the muse as other harbors. There can be, finally, no wholeness or Unity of Being without the other, but to attain that completion otherness must be invoked in its awful truth. Glory and loveliness do not return as the eye turns away; they do not return at all, as they were. But something like glory, a new beauty that includes sorrow, waits at the beams of the cross.

Needless to say, Endymion only begins the process. Even near the end of the fourth book, he cannot help admitting to the existence of doubts much like those that afflicted the narrator after the departure of the car in *Sleep and Poetry* (159–60). "Say," Endymion addresses his Indian, "is not bliss within our perfect seizure? / Oh, that I could not doubt" (IV, 720–21). Still necessarily divided in soul, Endymion needs both Indian and goddess, though the appearance of the Indian has made him reject the visionary voices that he sought earlier:

> No, never more
> Shall airy voices cheat me to the shore
> Of tangled wonder, breathless and aghast.
> [IV, 653–55]

One only stands "breathless" before the sublime, as the sonnet on *Chapman's Homer* suggests. Endymion has come to fear such breathlessness, however, and gives thanks to the Indian Maiden for redeeming his life "from too thin breathing" (IV, 650). What he wants is not to lose his own breath to the voice of otherness—as the speaker in the *Nightingale* ode asks Death to "take into the air my quiet breath"—because loss of breath is also loss of self and the possibility of one's own voice.

For Endymion the resolution of his dilemma of division comes rather rapidly and unexpectedly, with his submission to the will of heaven. He has already submitted to sorrow; with this second submission he precipitates the metamorphosis of the dark Indian to Cynthia. "Sister," he declares to Peona, "I would have command, / If it were heaven's will, on our sad fate."

> At which that dark-eyed stranger stood elate
> And said, in a new voice, but sweet as love,
> To Endymion's amaze: 'By Cupid's dove,
> And so thou shalt! And by the lily truth
> Of my own breast thou shalt, beloved youth!'
> And as she spake, into her face there came
> Light, as reflected from a silver flame.
>
> [IV, 977–83]

"A new voice, but sweet as love": by turning the cheating, airy voice to a voice of love Endymion seems to have completed successfully the quest begun so much earlier. Yet readers from the beginning have objected to the precipitousness of the close of the poem. Even so sympathetic a reader as Benjamin Bailey, in a letter to John Taylor written shortly after the publication of Keats's poem, could not avoid defending Keats's conclusion: "The 4th book, which I at first thought inferior, I *now* think as fine, & perhaps finer than any. You will stare at this. Nor do I think the abrupt conclusion so bad—it is *rather*, but not *much* too abrupt." [3] Among more recent critics, Harold Bloom sees the resolution of Endymion's dilemma as "desperate" and "mechanical," and Glen Allen and Stuart Sperry agree that the poet veered sharply from his original intentions.[4]

Keats too recognized a difficulty in concluding his myth. I mentioned earlier that the poet and Endymion began united; but by late in the fourth book the narrator intrudes upon his protagonist's quest in a troubling manner:

> Endymion! Unhappy! It nigh grieves
> Me to behold thee thus in last extreme:
> Ensky'd ere this, but truly that I deem
> Truth the best music in a first-born song.
>
> [IV, 770–73]

The poet's "truth" here contradicts the truth of the myth, as well as the "lily truth" that Cynthia offers Endymion as she becomes filled with light, in her transformation from the Indian Maiden. This is a central point in Keats's poetry, as

readers have noted, and we will return to it. But first, let us
go back to the invocation to the fourth book, which I think
begins the separation from the myth.

With Endymion safely returned to earth's "grassy nest" at
the close of book three, Keats begins his final book with an
invocation to the "Muse of my native land!" Pleased that he
could see at last the end of his long task, and pleased as well
with his opening, Keats wrote out the invocation (lines 1–29)
in a letter to Bailey (October 28, 1817). "You will see from
the Manner" of the lines, Keats writes, that "I had not an opportunity of mentioning any Poets, for fear of spoiling the
effect of the passage by particularising them!" Nevertheless,
the reader easily discerns references to the Bible, Dante and
Virgil, and Shakespeare as Keats traces the progress of
Poesy from the Hebrews to England. Yet perhaps more important to *Endymion* are the subtler presences of Milton and
Wordsworth at the beginning and end, respectively, of the
passage. Keats opens sublimely: his lofty muse, "first-born
on the mountains, by the hues / Of heaven on the spiritual
air begot" (2–3), recalls Milton's "holy light, offspring of
Heav'n first-born" (*Paradise Lost,* III, 1). But the passage
ends with Keats's recognition that the "Despondency" he
hoped to avoid by wreathing a band to earth nevertheless
besets all men.

> Long have I said, how happy he who shrives
> To thee! But then I thought on poets gone,
> And could not pray—nor could I now. So on
> I move to the end in lowliness of heart.
>
> [ll. 26–29]

Keats draws upon Wordsworth's *Resolution and Independence,*
in which the poet's "genial faith" is shaken by thoughts of
Chatterton's premature death and of the "despondency"
that comes in the end to poets. And he ends with the last line
of Wordsworth's *Lines, Left upon a Seat in a Yew-tree,* which
closes with an address to the man who wisely understands
that "True dignity abides with him alone / Who, in the silent

hour of inward thought, / Can still suspect, and still revere himself, / In lowliness of heart."

One might infer that this movement from a Miltonic sublimity to a Wordsworthian ideal of "true dignity" represents Keats's acceptance of a new model of poetry, one that fulfills the necessity, announced in the first book, of binding us "to the earth." But the substitution of poetic models does not solve the deeper problem of poetic despondency. When in the first book Keats found "joy" in a thing of beauty, he concluded that it could tie us to earth "Spite of despondence." Yet the invocation admits to the distressing continuation of this feeling: "Despondency besets / Our pillows, and the fresh tomorrow morn / Seems to give forth its light in very scorn / Of our dull, uninspired, snail-pacèd lives."

What emerges from this unsuccessful invocation is a situation in which the narrative of Endymion ironically completes the poet's own deprivation. Whereas, for example, the poet complains that the light of morning mocks our daily lives, Endymion finds that in Cynthia "a brighter day / Dawned" (IV, 985–86). Similarly, the light that in the invocation merely scorns our own poverty shows greater promise in the narrative, as it infuses Cynthia: Endymion watches as "into her face there came / Light" (IV, 982–83). A remarkable I-thou relation is being established between poet and protagonist, in which the poet is left on the shore of tangled wonder as Endymion receives the muse's gifts. What is involved, I think, is a matter of₁ belief: the truth of the myth runs counter to the poet's own beliefs. I would like to consider at this point the vicissitudes of poetic belief in Keats as they are reflected in his responses to other poets, especially Milton. Let us, therefore, take a brief excursus into Keats's reading, before returning to his own poetry.

EXCURSUS: KEATS'S MILTON

Keats read *Paradise Lost* in earnest during the winter of 1817–18, at the same time that he was concluding *Endymion*.

One of the best records we have of his reading during these
highly important months consists of the notes he made in his
two-volume edition of Milton that is now in the Keats House
in Hampstead.[5] In his rather extensive annotations Keats
suggests that Milton's natural inclination was toward moments of poetic "Luxury," the bliss of emotional satisfaction,
but that he was turned by feelings of "self-respect" that act
much like an ego ideal toward the "Ardours" of song—the
realm of the antithetical.

> The genius of Milton, more particularly in respect to
> its span in immensity, calculated him, by a sort of birth-
> right, for such an "argument" as the paradise lost. He
> had an exquisite passion for what is properly in the
> sense of ease and pleasure, poetical Luxury—and with
> that it appears to me he would fain have been content if
> he could so doing have preserved his self-respect and
> feel of duty perform'd—but there was working in him
> as it were that same sort of thing as operates in the great
> world to the end of a Prophesy's being accomplished—
> therefore he devoted himself rather to the Ardours
> than the pleasures of Song, solacing himself at intervals
> with cups of old wine—and these are with some excep-
> tions the finest parts of the Poem.[6]

In his previous reading of poetry also, we may note,
Keats's taste often had been selective. In one of his visits to
Enfield Academy, for example, he was more powerfully attracted to Spenser's dramatic and expressive epithets than to
the pervasive allegory of *The Faerie Queene*. In a well-known
remembrance, Charles Cowden Clarke recalls Keats's amazement upon reading a particular epithet: "He hoisted himself
up, and looked burly and dominant, as he said, 'what an
image that is—"sea-shouldering whales"!' " [7] And in a letter
to R. M. Milnes, Benjamin Bailey remembers that at Oxford
in September, 1817, Keats seemed to value Wordsworth
"rather in particular passages than in the full length portrait,
as it were, of the great imaginative & philosophic Christian
Poet, which he really is, & which Keats obviously, not long

afterwards, felt him to be." [8] In a similar manner, Keats came to believe that Milton's "Philosophy" might be "tolerably understood by one not much advanced in years" [9] and in his annotations responds with full empathy only to particular passages, usually those which on some level oppose the sublime freedom of heavenly or mythologized action to the mortal limitation of the self that is tied to recollection and literal seeing. He consistently describes his response to these passages in terms of the "pathos"—that is, the softening emotional quality—evoked by the compelling juxtaposition of these contrary states. Keats claims, for example, that Milton's portrait of the vale of the fallen angels is "among the most pathetic in the whole range of Poetry":

> *Others, more mild*
> *Retreated in a silent valley, sing*
> *With notes angelical to many a harp*
> *Their own heroic deeds and hapless fall*
> *By doom of battle;* and complain that Fate
> Free virtue should enthrall to force or chance.
> *Their song was partial, but the harmony*
> (What could it less when Spirits immortal sing?)
> *Suspended Hell,* and took with ravishment
> The thronging audience.[10]
> [*Paradise Lost,* II, 546–55; Keats's emphasis]

This moment of transport in the midst of otherwise inescapable signs of loss moves Keats to expand and deepen his earlier reference to the scene's "pathos": *"Milton is godlike in the sublime pathetic.* In Demons, fallen Angels, and Monsters the delicacies of passion, living in and from their immortality is of *the most softening and dissolving nature.* It is carried to the utmost here—Others more mild—nothing can express the sensation one feels at *'Their song was partial &c.'* " [11] The momentarily successful attempt by the fallen angels to erase the difference between possibility and desire, or fate and "virtue," engages and melts Keats's sense of self. The "softening and dissolving" sensation with which Keats responds to the pathos of the fallen angels is, I believe, directly paral-

lel to the Indian Maiden's love for the trapped Hyacinthus.
Like her, Keats is threatened with a loss of self that is a
direct result of loving, where what is loved has been made
desolate. Pathos is the sadness of self-surrender and includes
as well as sorrow a modicum of pride that one can love the
self in love, that though much has been lost there remains a
certain glory in the "delicacies of passion." Characteristically,
Keats responds to a literary image as though it were a truth
one feels on the pulses: he reads texts as life.

Keats's notes on *Paradise Lost* refer to instances in which
hope or desire is both partly victorious or largely defeated,
and though I shall argue for the greater importance to
Keats's own poetry of such defeats, it will be helpful to continue this brief examination of successful efforts in Milton to
satisfy desire. Keats's special sensitivity to moments in which
at great odds desire manages to suspend Hell is apparent in
his imagination's rush to other examples of them, each of
which involves a sense of struggle, or difficulty overcome.

> Examples of this nature are divine to the utmost in
> other poets—in Caliban *"Sometimes a thousand twangling
> instruments"* &c In Theocritus'—Polyphemus—and Ho-
> mer[']s Hymn to Pan when Mercury is represented as
> taking his *'homely fac'd'* to heaven There are numerous
> other instances in Milton—where Satan's progeny is
> called his *"daughter dear,"* and where this same Sin, a
> female, and with a feminine instinct for the showy and
> martial is in pain lest death should sully his bright arms,
> *'nor vainly hope to be invulnerable in those bright arms.'* [12]

Each of these "divine" examples represents the "sublime pathetic," the oxymoron Keats invents to describe the emotional duality in which a figure reaches out with love *though
in loss.* There is an acknowledgment in each instance, as in
the fourth book of *Endymion,* of the power of otherness to
bring desolation, yet each character retains the capacity to
humanize loss with love. In the Preface I cited Satan's obser-
vation of Adam and Eve as an example of reading a text in
terms of the dialectic of love, but Satan hesitated at the com-

mitment, halting at "could love." What so moves Keats is the oxymoronic quality in which "could love" yields to love: thus Satan's progeny is "dear" in the double Spenserian sense of lovable and costly. This duality obtains as Mercury proves greater than his child's limitation; as Caliban reveals an astonishing sensitivity to musical sound; as well as when Satan, though aware of the direct relation between Sin and his fall, transmutes regret to affection and declares her to be his "daughter dear." Passions like these are "delicate" because the mortality they shadow continually threatens to emerge and fully claim the self, and for this reason each self-realizing act is that much more precious, if that much more frail: "nor vainly hope to be invulnerable in those bright arms."

The contrary representation, in which the power of Hell is asserted *despite* the desire to love, evokes remarks by Keats of crucial importance and seems to achieve for him the stature of a truthful image of self. Whereas scenes of mortal circumstance partly overcome "are divine to the utmost in other poets," Milton's poem uniquely includes "two specimens of a very extraordinary beauty" which are "of a nature, so far as I have read, unexampled elsewhere—they are entirely distinct from the brief pathos of Dante. . . ." Keats cites the magnificent synecdoches which incarnate the myths of Proserpine and Orpheus:

> they are not to be found even in Shakespeare—they are according to the great prerogative of poetry better described in themselves than by a volume. The one is in the fol[lowing]—*'which cost Ceres all that pain'*—the other is that ending *'Nor could the Muse defend her son.'* [13]

Each of the lines in effect concludes Milton's allusion:

> Not that fair field
> Of *Enna* where *Proserpin* gath'ring flow'rs
> Herself a fairer Flow'r by gloomy *Dis*
> Was gather'd, which cost *Ceres* all that pain. . . .
>
> But drive far off the barbarous dissonance
> Of *Bacchus* and his Revellers, the Race

> Of that wild Rout that tore the *Thracian* Bard
> In *Rhodope,* where Woods and Rocks had Ears
> To rapture, till the savage clamor drown'd
> Both Harp and Voice; nor could the Muse defend
> Her Son.
>
> [*Paradise Lost,* IV, 268–71; VII, 32–38]

The ostensible intention of the first passage is to deprecate the pagan fields of Enna: Milton's completed statement concludes, "Not that fair field / Of *Enna* . . . might with this Paradise / Of *Eden* strive." That is, by the time we have read a few lines past the allusion to Enna, we discover that the neat symmetry of "that fair field / Of *Enna*" and "this Paradise / Of *Eden*" involves a contrast that elevates Eden—Enna could not compete with it. But the negation is suspended or momentarily arrested as Milton is drawn ever deeper into the circumstance of the classical myth. (Keats might call this a temporary abandonment of the "Ardours" for the "cups of old wine" of song.) Thus Milton adds depth to his mention of Enna by adumbrating a particular scene—"where *Proserpin* gath'ring flow'rs"; expands our understanding of the frailty of human beauty by juxtaposing "flowers" and "fair" with the epitome "Herself a fairer Flow'r"; and having created once more the loss in the field of Enna, finally reflects on Ceres. Keats says elsewhere in his annotations that Milton "sees Beauty on the wing, pounces upon it and gorges it to the producing his essential verse," [14] and this seems the case here.

The same intrusion of Milton's "luxurious" love of myth upon his narrative is evident in the second passage. The lines move inexorably toward the destruction of Orpheus, but as we proceed each clause creates a context for a reference in the preceding clause ("*Bacchus* and his Revellers, the Race / Of. . . ," "*Rhodope,* where . . ."), until, having passed through successive frames or portals, we sense the expansiveness and the saving relief of mythologized circumstance—"where Woods and Rocks had Ears / To rapture." Like Proserpine's beauty, the rapture Orpheus created lives again in Milton's poem and briefly suspends a movement toward loss.

But the redemptive power of myth, which is the power of plenitude and return, collapses in the final lines—those specifically noted by Keats—in which we abandon mythic possibility for the mortal perspective of Ceres and Calliope. The emotional descent from arrested continuity to a recognition that we are caught in successive time in effect describes a Fall in little, from the un-self-conscious innocence of Proserpine and Orpheus to a separate and isolated consciousness or awareness. Ceres and Calliope seem to be static witnesses to departure: they exist outside the frame of the mythic action, and Milton's unexpected turn to them reminds his reader of the inability of pagan myth to obviate the need for elegy, the poetic form in which the muse inevitably appears helpless. The two powerless mothers thus become figures of a "watchful care" like that of Endymion, for the loss of the objects of their love brings about a consciousness much like that of the "second self" that rises in Endymion. Each figure, writ large, would give us Moneta, whose unchanging watchfulness over a tragic scene represents a pure consciousness that is only a slight extension of those of Ceres and Calliope, as Keats reads them. Though Keats's empathy is with these female figures, the "Son" who could not be defended implies, however mutedly, an acknowledgment of the separation between Keats as poet and his own muse, who in the poetry increasingly displays an inability to defend her son.

When he annotated *Paradise Lost,* Keats regarded these passages as unique, but actually he had for some time valued similar poetic images of abatement and departure. Bailey recalls that at Oxford in September, 1817—while composing the third book of *Endymion*—Keats responded ardently to the close of Wordsworth's *She Dwelt Among the Untrodden Ways:* "The simplicity of the last line he declared to be the most perfect pathos."

> She lived unknown & few could know
> When Lucy ceased to be;

> But she is in her grave, & oh,
> The difference to me.[15]
>
> [Bailey's transcription]

And even earlier, Keats had felt upon the pulses this "difference" of separation. Charles Cowden Clarke states that "It was a treat to see as well as hear him read a pathetic passage." According to Clarke, Keats's eyes filled with tears while reading such a passage in *Cymbeline,* "and his voice faltered when he came to the departure of Posthumus, and Imogen, saying she would have watched him—

> till the diminution
> Of space had pointed him sharp as my needle;
> Nay follow'd him till he had melted from
> *The smallness of a gnat to air;* and then
> Have turn'd mine eye and wept." [16]

Like Endymion listening to the song "O Sorrow," Keats as poet is found by these images of loss, in which what one loves slips away despite his love. Imogen does not turn her eye to find the replenishment that the poet found in *I Stood Tip-toe,* she turns to weep her loss. In a sense we have a poetic situation that is equivalent to that characteristic circumstance in Gray in which the speaker finds he has lost the world despite his love for it. This—in both cases—is "pathos," but it is not the "sublime pathetic," in which the character overcomes the consequent frozenness and manages to open out to the power of otherness in a renewed gesture of love. Here, both the speaker in Wordsworth's poem and Imogen share a common perspective with Ceres and Calliope. All are made aware of cessation by suffering the loss of vital figures. We sense a consequent vulnerability, an openness to the power of space to diminish or of the underworld to reach out unexpectedly, heightened by each observer's seeming powerlessness and immobility—which contrasts with the receding movement of those lost. In each passage he cites, Keats's sympathy is evoked less by the lost figure, whose existence in *Paradise Lost* and in Wordsworth's poem tends to be mythicized and hence removed from temporality, than by the circumstance of the remaining character. Keats's powerful empathy acutely recognizes the "pathos" that attends the return to historical time of Wordsworth's speaker and Calliope and of Ceres and Imogen, and in their situations Keats appears to discover a truth of separation that parallels the narrator's "truth" in *Endymion,* which refutes Cynthia's promise of union in the skies.

For Milton, however, the pagan myths of Proserpine and Orpheus are examples of fable. Though his imagination seems unable to avoid extending the moment, thereby briefly suppressing the irrevocability of Fall, there is nothing in either outcome to suggest that Ceres or Calliope can hope for redemption. The synecdoches thus contrast with the Fall of Adam and Eve and its aftermath, in which the survival of creation is guaranteed by God's grace.[17] In book eleven, Adam views man's future as a series of falls which variously invite catastrophe. Adam here is in much the same position as Ceres or Calliope, but at his worst moments he is sustained by the demonstrated sufficiency of the just man. Nevertheless, after the Flood the narrative is broken by an intrusion that is remarkably uncharacteristic of Milton's usual remove:

How did'st thou grieve then, *Adam,* to behold
The end of all thy Offspring, end so sad,
Depopulation; thee another Flood,
Of tears and sorrow a Flood thee also drown'd,
And sunk thee as thy Sons.

[XI, 754–58]

Neil H. Hertz has convincingly argued the singularity of Milton's intrusion and the manner by which his sympathy is evoked by the grieving figure of Adam, even though that sympathy by implication denies the hope of Christian forgiveness.[18] Momentarily, Adam seems to Milton as forlorn as Ceres or Calliope ("So fail not thou," Milton implored his own muse after remarking Calliope's inadequacy). Milton's intentions, we assume, were not to jeopardize the status of his Guarantor. And, in fact, the usual observer *ab extra* in *Paradise Lost* is made aware of the strength of virtue, of a power that will not fail him.[19] But Keats responds to Ceres and Calliope very much as Milton responds to Adam during this moment in which loss seems irredeemable. Milton's own bereavement at Adam's tears suggests an empathy that finds a precise parallel in the tears Clarke observed, in the tears of the Indian Maiden, and in Keats's deeply felt responses to the passages in Wordsworth and Milton. Though Milton, Keats writes, "committed himself to the Extreme"—that is, to the antithetical—Keats has read *Paradise Lost* as if his great precursor were a poet of the "sublime pathetic" rather than the sublime, and by so doing has made the oxymoron of loss and gain in the dialectic of love the proper subject of modern poetry.

Keats probably annotated his edition of Milton some time between January 27—the date of Hazlitt's influential lecture on Milton—and April 27, 1818, when he wrote to Reynolds that he longed "to feast upon old Homer as we have upon Shakespeare and as I have lately upon Milton." [20] As is frequently the case, Hazlitt's views and terminology seem to have influenced strongly Keats's reading of Milton. The lecture "On Shakspeare and Milton" was the third in a series on the English poets that Hazlitt delivered at the Surrey Institution. Hazlitt finds great "pathos" in the portrait of Satan and in the loss of Eden to Adam and Eve; but in this brief examination I would like to glance at his comment on the fallen angels—the same passage Keats annotates in his copy of Milton. "But, perhaps, of all the passages of Paradise Lost," Hazlitt declares, "the description of the employments of the angels during the absence of Satan, some of whom 'retreated in a silent valley, sing with notes angelical to many a harp their own heroic deeds and hapless fall by doom of battle,' is the most perfect example of mingled pathos and sublimity." [21] Keats turns this to the "sublime pathetic," shifting the balance in favor of a constraint that is touched by redemption, as beauty, in the forthcoming *Hyperion,* is replaced in the poet's eyes by a beautiful sorrow, or as Cynthia-as-goddess yields to the Indian Maiden as an object of sympathy. The dates of Keats's annotations seem very likely, a fact of importance when we consider that most of the fourth book of *Endymion* was composed in October and November, 1817, and the corrections made in March, 1818.

If we now return to the relation of narrator to hero in *Endymion* we can see certain parallels to Keats's reading. After the apologetic lines about the delay in enskying Endymion, the poet continues his address, and adds to the distance between himself and his character:

> Yes, moonlight Emperor! Felicity
> Has been thy meed for many thousand years;
> Yet often have I, on the brink of tears,
> Mourn'd as if yet thou wert a forester;—
> Forgetting the old tale.
>
> > [IV, 776–80]

Keats responds to Endymion as though he were as undefended a son as Orpheus, and as if the myth culminated in the defeat of the desire to be sublimed. As a consequence, the poet is able to assume a posture identical to that of the figures that remained to face mortality in the "pathetic" scenes he admires: on those widening, human shores stand Ceres and Calliope, and like them he "on the brink of tears" acknowledges the inability of ecstasy and the sublime—the "felicity" of timelessness and discontinuity—to console a human audience. These are the tears shed by Imogen, and by Keats in reading of her, against winter visions. Keats has repeated the Miltonic collapse from a mythologized realm, though to do so he has had to arrest the progress of his myth by the consciously artificial expedient of "forgetting" its outcome. And his reference to that myth—his own subject—as an "old tale" makes the narrative of Endymion an illusion with no future; belief now has shifted to the "forester," who evokes emotions appropriate to elegy. The movement from the myth of Endymion to a new sphere of "truth" begins with the negation of "Yet," which for the moment halts the progress of the myth and proffers an alternative region of possibility:

> Yet often have I, on the brink of tears,
> Mourn'd as if yet thou wert a forester.

Keats's avowal of loss directly parallels those assertions in which Milton underlines the failure of pagan myth—"which cost *Ceres* all that pain." Milton's deprecation of myth is consonant with his desire to set forth the greater truth of a higher argument. But Keats affirms not an orthodoxy (insofar as we may attribute one to Milton), but a paradigm of existence, generally felt rather than deduced, and encountered in his reading of Milton and other poets.

> Felicity
> Has been *thy* meed for many thousand years;
> Yet often have *I*, on the brink of tears,
> Mourned.
>
> [IV, 776–78; my emphasis]

Posed against the achieved good fortune of Endymion is the speaker's own melancholy; he is not beyond the "brink of recollection" but "on the brink of tears," for the power of enchantment has not been sufficient to create a genuine moment of origin. A very similar opposition, in which the speaker assumes the perspective of observer *ab extra* with regard to an object or symbol of a fulfilled quest, informs much of Keats's poetry after *Endymion,* and often, we may note in concluding this section, can be seen at the heart of the visionary experience itself: "Still wouldst thou sing, and I have ears in vain."

"HYPERION": SEEING FEELINGLY

We began this chapter with a statement of the dilemma a poet faces in appropriating to himself the power to renounce the bliss so widely sought in post-Miltonic poetry. Emotionally, that sensual happiness is an intimation of a kind of immortality, since its presence opposes any losses of the object—any "disappointment," as Yeats says, that creates antithetical poets. Yeats feels that the necessity of renunciation arises inevitably, as perhaps it does, at least temporarily, since retention of objects tends to tie consciousness to the past. Keats, we recall, associates literal sight with memory. The sorrow that the Indian Maiden sees in love lengthens to the pathos Keats sees in Calliope and Imogen; both emotions effect a desire to hold on to what is slipping away, to retain a relationship that is passing. The reason that the motheral figures appear so static is that they have been frozen, in a way, by the movement into history of those they have loved. The "freedom" that Glaucus, Endymion, and, in book four, the narrator seek is a form of discontinuity that absolves the self of such an imprisonment. Keats intellectually recognizes the necessity of that freedom and the corresponding necessity of renunciation, but emotionally he feels the truth of the self tied to passing things—man is in love, and he loves what fades, Yeats writes.

From this view, the translation that is intrinsic to the myth of Endymion and the moon is a false possibility, or perhaps we should say, an emotionally unacceptable one. Yet the poet's goal, of making it possible for himself to love, remains. This is where the question of belief plays so central a role, for there can be no relationship without some belief. Milton's belief, Keats thought, was reflected in his having committed himself to the extreme that is the antithetical, which made it possible for the poet to give up those cups of old wine that, Keats insists, are still the best parts of *Paradise Lost*. Unable so to commit himself, and equally unable to retain his belief in the principle of beauty sought in his own earlier poems, Keats turns to the myth of the fall of the Titans as a means of discovering a more truthful beauty that may reflect the ambivalence rather than the extreme of experience, and so represent a tentative faith if not full belief. *Hyperion,* that is, seeks the experential equivalent of the oxymoron, the place of choice to which the daemon leads the poet who has given up simpler belief.

Keats's poetic strategy, if we may so designate it, continues

the departure from literal vision begun in *Endymion.* Only in
Hyperion it is not a new voice that we hear, it is a new form of
seeing that tells us something about Keats's still emerging
poetic beliefs. Shelley, in his extraordinary and beautiful
essay *A Defence of Poetry,* claims that the great task of poetry
is to rescue the universe from the deadness of successive
time so that we may regard it properly once more: poetry
"creates anew the universe, after it has been annihilated in
our minds by the recurrence of impressions blunted by reiteration," and in doing so it "compels us to *feel* that which we
perceive." [22] As Keats increases his commitment to sorrow he
affirms this approach, in which one perceives feelingly and
thereby rescues not only the world but the emotional self,
which is threatened with annulment by the ecstasy of the
sublime. Morris Dickstein points out [23] that Keats recoiled
from the effort of *Endymion* by composing on its heels the
very different poem *In Drear-Nighted December,* which asserts
that no man ever lived who "Writhed not of passèd joy,"
nor, the poem continues, could there be expressed in poetry
"The feel of not to feel it."

The feel of feeling (Richard Woodhouse, by the way, objected to Keats's use of the word "feel" for "feeling") seems
to have a good deal to do with self-acceptance, which is now
an acceptance of the self in its vulnerability. This I think is
one consequence of Keats's reading of Milton and others, or
rather of the sensibility behind the reading. Still, if the dynamic of reading (in its broad sense) that I have sketched
holds true, too much feeling will cause the poet to be only a
reader, and so make him desolate. This is how Saturn appears at the opening of *Hyperion,* fallen into his doleful vale
and "quiet as a stone, / Still as the silence round about his
lair" (I, 4–5). Silence has overtaken the ruler of the Titans,
who has memories of his godhead but now progresses toward a state much like human mortality. As he reflects on
the sudden displacement that brought about his present
woe, he inadvertently seems to supply the reason for it that
he seeks:

> Who had power
> To make me desolate? Whence came the strength?
> How was it nurtured to such bursting forth,
> While Fate seemed strangled in my nervous grasp?
> But it is so; and I am smothered up,
> And buried from all godlike exercise
> Of influence benign on planets pale,
> Of admonitions to the winds and seas,
> Of peaceful sway above man's harvesting,
> And all those acts which Deity supreme
> Doth ease its heart of love in.
>
> [I, 102–12]

The myth of the Titans calls for Saturn's disposession by a "power," as he says, greater than his own. But there is something inevitable about his fall, something in his nature which leads inexorably to loss of heaven, and the Titans who speak in the great council recognize this, regardless of how their particular explanations differ. Traditional readings of the poem see Saturn, a powerful god with a strong identity, necessarily replaced by Keats's poetic ideal, the god without identity or character, represented by Apollo. We do the poem wrong, however, to reduce it to the apparent philosophy of the letters, helpful as these are. Saturn's fall is personal as well as representative and follows from the nature of his godhead: in easing his heart of love he falls victim to the danger faced by poets as well—he surrenders self without retaining power or self-possession. Saturn is overtaken by his own simple expression of love, for this (for both gods and poets) is the easier way—with the consequence, however, of the loss of one's proper realm.

I mentioned that *Hyperion* seeks the fullness of oxymoron. Saturn's loving but innocent relation to outer things, including earth, represents a dangerous, partial statement that invites usurpation by the power that makes one desolate. Milton presents this situation as a ravishment that takes away the ability to reply, or a higher strain that silences response.

Thus, in *Comus,* Silence "Was took ere she was ware." Keats modifies Milton's portrayal of what in ideal form would be a "perfect Diapason": Saturn is taken by otherness in *Hyperion* precisely because he has loved. The consequence of this sympathy is his silence, the loss of poetic voice.

It is apparent that I am reading *Hyperion* on one level as an allegory of poetic incarnation, which may strike readers as an unnecessary narrowing of focus. One might argue the contrary, however, for considerations of identity and fall move quickly from the personal to the universal. Moreover, Keats himself tended to examine the problems of good and evil in terms of their representations in poetry, as his letters repeatedly indicate. *"Hyperion,"* Stuart Sperry argues, "like most of Keats's longer poems, is on one level concerned with poetry and the various degrees of its power. . . ." In addition, Sperry finds that it "was only natural for Keats, in working toward the criterion of tragic beauty appropriate to his own age, to begin by crystallizing a sense of the failure of the generation of poets before his own." Sperry consequently sees in the portrait of Hyperion features much like Wordsworth's, the older contemporary against whom Keats measured himself.[24]

Sperry's reading is suggestive: it is difficult not to see a parallel between Saturn's former "strong identity" (I, 114) and the "wordsworthian or egotistical sublime" that Keats disparages in a letter to Woodhouse on October 27, 1818. There are, nevertheless, other presences haunting the figure of Saturn, and these add to the significance of his experience. He is first presented to us as "Far sunken from the healthy breath of morn, / Far from the fiery noon, and eve's one star" (I, 2–3). Removed from morn, noon, evening: has Keats not subtly limned Milton into the portrait, the Milton who in his blindness complained that "not to me returns / Day, or the sweet approach of Ev'n or Morn" (*Paradise Lost,* III, 41–42)? The next logical question is, Why associate Saturn with the blind Milton, who as the model for the general theme of Keats's poem we would not expect to see in a fallen character? The answer, I believe, has to do with

Keats's metaphoric use of blindness, as we encountered this in *Endymion,* and perhaps also with his defensive strategy against his great precursor.

Keats, as we know, protested the egoism of the "wordsworthian" sublime, because to him it represented an extraordinary quantity of self-possession or sense of identity that mitigates sympathy. Keats's own evolving ideal is the negative capability we noted earlier, in which the poet evinces the capability of remaining neutral to the agencies acting upon him. This stated ideal is consonant with the character of the poet proper that Keats wrote of as a contrast to the Wordsworthian poet. The poet Keats admires has no identity, as he writes Woodhouse on October 27, 1818—probably the same month he began *Hyperion:* "A Poet is the most unpoetical of any thing in existence; because he has no Identity. . . ." [25] Yet by the following spring Keats writes of the world as a "vale of Soul-making" that fosters the growth of the *"Soul* or *Intelligence destined to possess the sense of Identity."* [26] The ideal of the identity-less poet thus barely survives the period of the composition of the poem (Keats seems to have abandoned it in April, 1819); and the poem seems to endorse the ideal far less than we are used to thinking. Negative capability comes to mean, not the absence of identity, but the more moving situation of a partial surrender of identity to the power of otherness—an act of love that makes possible the sublime pathos of poetic reply.

The other may come to blind, then, but its threat makes possible the poet's own voice, as Milton's "wakeful bird sings darkling." Wallace Stevens touches this felt perception in *Peter Quince at the Clavier,* in which he concludes that "Music is feeling, then, not sound." Blindness is not only Oedipal, as the other threatens to appear as the sphinx, but is also a form of antithetical completion that gives to the merely literal the "depth" the soul requires (a reiterated metaphor in *Endymion*). Keats, still resisting the antithetical, blinds (in a manner) Saturn, with implications we shall consider. But let us first cast a glance at blindness in *King Lear,* which Keats had read again and annotated in January, 1818, and for which he wrote a sonnet. Blindness in the play is curiously rewarding, in the antithetically compensatory way we have discussed:

> *Lear.* Your eyes are in a heavy case, your purse in a light; yet you see how this world goes.
> *Gloucester.* I see it feelingly.
>
> [IV, vi, 144–47]

Though we shall be considering the similar relation of sight and feeling in the portrait of Saturn, I am not suggesting the direct "influence" of Gloucester's words on Keats, despite his close reading of the play and the obvious indebtedness of Saturn to the general portrait of Lear. Yet the conjunction of seeing and feeling in the play must have struck Keats as an expression of some of his own thoughts, concerned as he was at this time with the consolations of pathetic situations. Pathos might be described as blind feeling, the surrender of self to a perceived condition of loss that brings no compensatory inflooding of vision. Saturn, the god who surrendered self in acts of love (even though that "self" might have been naively egotistical), *felt without seeing,* and his recognition of the goddess Thea is therefore tinged with a pathetic tenderness, but not with the sublime pathetic:

> O tender spouse of gold Hyperion,
> Thea, I *feel* thee ere I *see* thy face.
>
> [I, 95–96; my emphasis]

Readers will think at this point of Moneta's removing her veils and discovering her face to the poet's sight in the revised *The Fall of Hyperion.* But during the time he is writing the earlier poem, Keats is still working toward the momentary perfection of relationship in which love overcomes fear, in the fullness of lyrical experience that is self's experience with everything that seems beyond itself. *Hyperion* weaves both Lear and Milton into the image of Saturn's blind feeling in a subtle complaint against loss in love: "thee I revisit safe," as Milton invokes the holy light that is his muse, "And *feel* thy sovran vital Lamp; but thou / Revisit'st not these eyes" (III, 21–23; my emphasis). Milton ends his invocation with a prayer for inward vision, "that I may see and tell / Of things invisible to mortal sight" (ll. 54–55), but Saturn's sight is unpurged, and he passes the time in a "slumbrous solitude" (I, 69) or a lulling that is sleep, not poetry.

With his fall, Saturn like Glaucus discovers irony, the trope that depends upon displacements in time and meaning. Saturn desires a parity between his present circumstance and the heaven he remembers; but as Thea sadly observes, the earth does not know him as a god. Like Lear, he insists that "Saturn must be King," that "there must be a golden victory" (I, 125, 126).

> Voices of soft proclaim, and silver stir
> Of strings in hollow shells; and there shall be
> Beautiful things made new, for the surprise
> Of the sky-children.
>
> [I, 130–33]

If beautiful things could be made new one could make an identity of past and present—an identity that would obviate irony. There are no beautiful things that are joys forever in *Hyperion,* only this desire to preserve what is actually lost, to make it possible for the mind to retain objects. Thus would nature be saved for the mind, and thus both Wordsworth and Yeats, as we have seen, construe a binding as the working of the natural or emotional imagination. Saturn's desire is the reflex of the loss Ceres and Calliope also suffer, and suggests the tie to the past that results from such pathos. This is why emotional desire invokes sublimation rather than the repression that is necessary to antithetical imaginings: sublimation is a means of preserving a relationship that repression blocks. Saturn's wish is for the "again" of emotional completion, the return of beautiful things "made new." But ironically, Hyperion (who still holds his position in heaven, though shakily) discovers that for the Titans there can be only "horrors new" (I, 233).

As is usual in representations of fallenness in Keats, the Titans become subject to successive time rather than the rep-

etition that Saturn craves. Thea vainly attempts to waken
Saturn from sleep and false dreaming but realizes that she
might do better to protect him from her awareness of the
truth of continuous time:

> O aching time! O moments big as years!
> All as ye pass swell out the monstrous truth,
> And press it so upon our weary griefs
> That unbelief has not a space to breathe.
>
> [I, 64–67]

Thea cannot but believe that the moments "pass" irretriev-
ably, a fact that informs a long, extended simile that follows:

> As when, upon a trancèd summer night,
> Those green-robed senators of mighty woods,
> Tall oaks, branch-charmèd by the earnest stars,
> Dream, and so dream all night without a stir,
> Save from one gradual solitary gust
> Which comes upon the silence, and dies off,
> As if the ebbing air had but one wave;
> So came these words and went.
>
> [I, 72–79]

Saturn is one of these oaks that have been charmed or enchanted into silence by a star that appears "earnest," but he
does not realize that there is no way to recall the time. The
air ebbs as if it has but one wave, and that is flowing from
him. Against the "gust / which comes upon the silence, and
dies off," we might view the Lady's song in *Comus,* which
creates "raptures" that "float upon the wings / Of silence." In
a way we can consider Saturn, a figure out of the Miltonic
sublime, as charmed by the "earnest" promise of that song,
only to discover that it has ebbed from him, that the wave
was singular. The Lady in *Comus* sings her song to Echo, but
for Saturn there are no echoes of Thea's words, nor do they
ring with strains that create souls under the ribs of death.

While Saturn sleeps, unaware of time passing, an astonishing and authentic metamorphosis is taking place.
There is of course the creation of Apollo over in the next

county, as it were, but I mean here the change in Thea, a
change so radical as to make heaven merely the shadow of
earth:

> Her face was large as that of Memphian sphinx,
> Pedestalled haply in a palace court,
> When sages looked to Egypt for their lore.
> But oh, how unlike marble was that face!
> How beautiful, if sorrow had not made
> Sorrow more beautiful than Beauty's self.
>
> [I, 31–36]

In this remarkable description, Keats makes sorrow the vehicle by which beauty is rescued from the past—not beautiful
things made new, but the sorrow of beauty that is still felt.
The sphinx simile suggests that Thea was marble and was
sphinxlike in her distance from the poet, and from us in the
present: she existed "When sages looked to Egypt," and like
the Queen-Moon in the *Nightingale* ode she is "haply" on her
throne, which is in a region the poet cannot reach. There is
just a hint here of the distance of Cynthia, which Keats earlier evaded. Here he does not evade, he takes upon himself
the burden of the threat of the sphinx, the muse who like
Milton's Melancholy has forgotten herself to marble; and he
brings her into his human sphere by humanizing her with a
sorrow that is his as well as hers. This is not, I think, so full a
measure of self-recognition and outward love as we find in
the later version of the poem, but it is a definite and powerful instance of the poet's acceptance of sorrow making possible his reaching out to the other who is out of reach. As the
sublime pathetic replaces the sublime for Keats, so this sorrowful beauty replaces earlier things of beauty, and every
subsequent reference to beauty in the poem—including
Oceanus's important claim that beauty and might are al-
lied—must be viewed in the context of this new ideal.

The humanization of the sublime that begins with Thea
depends upon fallenness, and particularly on an acceptance
of this, which is an acceptance of one's own diminution.
Hyperion, the one Titan who is yet unfallen, cannot know

this partial victory. All around him, however, are signs of the imminence of his dethronement, to which he responds by attempting to hold on to his "sovereignty" (I, 165), a word that Oceanus repeats tellingly. Hyperion's version of sovereignty, like Endymion's "sovereign vision," is threatened by the power of the sublime other, which the Titan tries vainly to oppose. As a result he contemplates a blinding that he interprets as the expression of the other's domination of him:

> Even here, into my centre of repose,
> The shady visions come to domineer,
> Insult, and blind.
>
> [I, 243–45]

"Fall?" Hyperion asks, and provides his own answer: "No, by Tellus and her briny robes!" Hyperion interprets the threat of domination as requiring a stubborn resistance that might effect a change in the unfolding of events. Thus he attempts to circumvent the coming darkness by beginning day early, but such a discontinuity is impossible: "Fain would he have commanded, fain took throne / And bid the day begin, if but for change" (I, 290–91).

Hyperion's resistance is an error from the perspective of negative capability and human sorrow. Though he is still a god, of course, and shall always be one, he tends more and more to resemble the frail men for whose benefit he once drove the chariot of the sun. His own fire is becoming diminished to mortal intensity and merely mortal power: "His flaming robes streamed out beyond his heels, / And gave a roar, as if of earthly fire" (I, 214–15). That for the poet is perhaps all the fire there is, but Hyperion chooses to follow his father Coelus's advice and *oppose* his "ethereal presence" to "each malignant hour," rather than surrender to the power of darkness. This is positive instead of negative capability, an irritable reaching out rather than a submission that is love, and we consequently have our doubts about the wisdom of Hyperion's response to the darkness that is so like death:

> Am I to leave this haven of my rest,
> This cradle of my glory, this soft clime,
> This calm luxuriance of blissful light,
> These crystalline pavillions and pure fanes
> Of all my lucent empire? It is left
> Deserted, void, nor any haunt of mine.
> The blaze, the splendour and the symmetry
> I cannot see—but darkness, death and darkness.
>
> [I, 235–42]

This moving speech, which mingles memories of Eve's hymn to night and her lament for the paradise she must leave, is nevertheless a mistaken response, as is indicated by a comparison of Hyperion's "I cannot see" with the similar line of the speaker in the *Nightingale* ode, "I cannot see what flowers are at my feet." The speaker in the ode has loved (or half-loved) the darkness and won plenitude from it, but Hyperion sees only death—this is his blindness, which is partly a result of a failure to submit. Hyperion is as much imprisoned as Glaucus or Endymion were and has as little chance of being the source of his own salvation. But like them he chooses to dive for freedom, to risk all on a change of element, in the hope that the darkness that seems death may yield the surprise of " 'twas to live." Endymion compared himself to "one / Who dived three fathoms . . . in beds of coral"; Hyperion appears "Like to a diver in the pearly seas" as he "plunged all noiseless into the deep night" (I, 355, 357), the bourne from which no falling traveler returns.

The significance of the fall of the Titans is debated in the great council by two antipodal speakers, Oceanus and Clymene. Oceanus's view, to which a number of readers have attached great significance, finds a "balm" in the "truth" of a universal progress toward perfection. By drastically curtailing both self-consciousness and desire, Oceanus is able to welcome the "power more strong in beauty" that has replaced the Titans:

> Say, doth the dull soil
> Quarrel with the proud forests it hath fed,

> And feedeth still, more comely than itself?
> Can it deny the chiefdom of green groves?
> Or shall the tree be envious of the dove
> Because it cooeth, and hath snowy wings
> To wander wherewithal and find its joys?
>
> [II, 217–23]

On this basis, Oceanus proclaims a principle of succession that he hopes will provide consolation to the mourning Titans: " 'tis the eternal law / That first in beauty should be first in might" (II, 228–29). This argument is persuasive but partial, and we should not view it as Keats's own. Oceanus views history as impersonal progress. He abstracts the self from successive time, and by so doing is able to consider even his own fall without pathos. Beauty for him is the beauty of the old sublime, of "might half slumbering on its own right arm," as *Sleep and Poetry* describes Poesy. But this is a definition that for the poet has been changed by the advent of sorrow which, as we have seen, has become more beautiful than beauty's self. Thea's transfiguration suggests death as the mother of beauty; Oceanus's self-renunciation moves him to the antithetical only, where beauty is absolute and external—an intellectual beauty in its extreme form. His argument is therefore terribly abstract: "Sophist and sage," Oceanus is an early version of Apollonius in *Lamia,* who also is both "sophist" and "sage" (II, 291; I, 375), but who unweaves the rainbow of poetry.

Clymene, on the other hand, is a simple elegiast, all of whose "knowledge" is summarized in the statement that "joy is gone" (II, 253). Hers is the voice of pathos; she sings feelingly but without self-possession. As she stood in grief upon a shore, she tells us, a sweet clime drifted toward her. "Full of calm joy it was, as I of grief; / *Too* full of joy and soft delicious warmth" (II, 265–66; my emphasis). This is a Spenserian reduction by repetition. Fradubio in *The Faerie Queene* turns on his love for Fraelissa in the same way: "And to this wretched Lady, my dear love, / O *too* dear love, love bought with death too dear" (I, ii, 31; my emphasis). Clymene, that

is, closes herself to the sublime, as Fradubio does to Fraelissa. As a consequence, she dooms herself to mere pathos
and the *false* (one might say, dubious) oxymoron of a "living
death":

> There came enchantment with the shifting wind,
> That did both drown and keep alive my ears.
> I threw my shell away upon the sand,
> And a wave filled it, as my sense was filled
> With that new blissful golden melody.
> A living death was in each gush of sounds,
> Each family of rapturous hurried notes,
> That fell, one after one, yet all at once.
>
> [II, 276–83]

With ears to rapture, Clymene is taken by the higher
strains of Olympian music, which seems to come both succes-
sively ("one after one") and simultaneously ("yet all at
once")—both continuously and discontinuously. This is authentic "new"-ness, which both drowns and revitalizes, as the
voice of love in *Endymion* had power to confound heaven
and earth into paradox. The Indian Maiden recognized that
this voice demanded "meek surrender," but she preserved
herself against total loss of self by her tears, which beto-
kened her sorrow. Clymene loses self in a "living death"
which, however sensual, is no more desirable than Moneta's
situation—"deathwards progressing / To no death."

Keats presumably intended Apollo to unite the power of
Oceanus with the pathos of Clymene, and thus to demonstrate the passing from anterior to present gods, and perhaps from previous to contemporary poets. Whereas Saturn
vainly sought beautiful things made new and Hyperion ironically met horrors new, Mnemosyne tells Apollo that she has
abandoned the Titans "For prophecies of thee, and for the
sake / Of loveliness new born" (III, 78–79). This more-than-
Wordsworthian loveliness escapes the curse of passingness:
we recall that Keats's dedicatory sonnet to his 1817 volume
complained that loveliness has passed away. Apollo's birth is
thus for the poet a rebirth, but one that brings another

order of beauty. The new god overcomes the error of Titanic existence with the help of a great influx of knowledge—"Knowledge enormous makes a God of me," he cries out (III, 113). Thus prepared, he undergoes an agony of transformation in which he passes from innocence, through the portals of death, to godhead, a process that culminates in his oxymoronic dying "into life." This is the exact reverse of Clymene's unhappy "living death," and so the god is born into a more modern perspective, in which death is a part of awareness.

But when Apollo does indeed "Die into life" (III, 130), is it the life of man or god? One of the problems Keats seems to have had in continuing the poem—it breaks off just after this point—seems to be that it is difficult to bestow an earthly sensibility on undying gods. Mnemosyne, who shares the Titans' inability to appreciate the necessity of sorrow, implores the Olympian god, "Tell me, youth, / What sorrow thou canst feel," thus indicating the gap between early and present divinity (and previous and contemporary poets). Apollo thus has all the necessary attributes for the love that humanizes ghostly otherness, except that he himself is now the ghost. When Keats goes on to revise the fragment, he will put himself into this role; but the first *Hyperion* has the curious problem of a god who combines sorrow and beauty, pathos and the sublime, but with no existential correlatives for the mortal shadings.

Keats, however, provides his own reasons for terminating the fragment, and these have to do with style. "I have given up Hyperion," Keats writes to J. H. Reynolds on September 21, 1819. "There were too many Miltonic inversions in it—Miltonic verse cannot be written but in an artful or rather artist's humour. I wish to give myself up to other sensations." As the date suggests, Keats doubtless was referring to the revised version of the poem. But as Bate observes, the earlier version is actually more full of inversions than the later; moreover, Bate continues, Reynolds "did not have a copy of the *Fall,* only of the first *Hyperion;* and Keats, in suggesting that Reynolds look over the poem again, is referring to the first *Hyperion*." [27] We may infer then that the early version of the poem presented the difficulties that could not be solved by revision, and Keats's complaint about the excessive Miltonic style certainly applies to both versions.

Recent readers have viewed the stylistic problem in the broader context of what Geoffrey Hartman calls the "objective mode" of the poem, a mode in which the poet is notably absent.[28] Hartman finds a causative relation between the motheral identities of the muse-figures in the poem—Thea and Mnemosyne—and "the suppressed self of the poet." Hartman is too subtle a critic to attribute the style of the poem entirely to a desire for maternal presence, and I refer the reader to his essay for his explanation of the interrelation of "the spectral mother, the idea of nurture and a concept of language." Proceeding from a similar assumption— that the style of the poem, especially of the first two books, is Miltonic, objective, an attempt at the old, high sublime—I would like to take up this problem of the self-curtailment of the poet. There are, in fact, two voices in the poem that call for just such a posture: those of Oceanus and Coelus. Oceanus attempts to convey an understanding of proper "sovereignty" to the fallen Titans as a consolation for their having fallen: "Now comes the pain of truth, to whom 'tis pain— / O folly! for to bear all naked truths, / And to envisage circumstance, all calm, / That is the top of sovereignty" (II, 202–05). Pain is a part of self-consciousness in this formulation, and to purge one removes the other as well. A less drastic but still purgative call for objectivity is implicit in Coelus's fears for his child, Hyperion, whom he sees growing increasingly like mortal men.

> Unruffled, like high Gods, ye lived and ruled.
> Now I behold in you fear, hope, and wrath;
> Actions of rage and passion—even as
> I see them, on the mortal world beneath,
> In men who die.
>
> [I, 331–35]

Coelus's faith is in "Manifestations of that beauteous life / Diffused unseen throughout eternal space" (I, 317–18). For "beauteous life" Keats's manuscript originally had "Life and Beauty": Coelus's mighty abstract principle centers on a beauty that knows no sorrow, that exists apart from men who die, and that survives them.

Both Coelus and Oceanus urge "The feel of not to feel it," the abstractions that avoid emotion and passion, and self-consciousness. If Keats's style is an attempt to express their idea of sovereignty, we may ask why it does so, when the sorrowful beauty of Thea seems to represent an advance over impersonal beauty. It may be that Keats's apparent rejection of emotion stems from the pain of nursing Tom through the last stages of his illness: Keats's younger brother died on December 1, 1818, affecting the poet deeply. But biographical explanations carry us only part of the way. Nor can we look to Apollo's incarnation as an alternative to the objective mode. It is true that the style changes in the fragment of book three that we have, but Apollo's deification depends upon an influx of knowledge, and knowledge controls, names, and is in general a form of power, not subjectivity.

No, I think we must go back to Saturn and pathos and the tragedy of loving to come to terms even partly with the style of the poem. Saturn's loss in love seems to be a source of anxiety for the poet, who responds by identifying Saturn with Lear and with Milton as the precursor, and Apollo, who because of the grand march of intellect has acquired protective knowledge, with the modern poet. Apollo is a saving alternative to Saturn, when what is needed really is an ethos that builds upon Saturn's human experience. No knowledge will console for the fact that women have cancers, as Keats knew, and no speculations on existence can afford to ignore pathos. Nevertheless, Keats, fearing vulnerability, as poet renounces human emotion and passion and purges the poem of the "I" of the speaker, for this always is the emotional "I" that reaches out to the intellectual daemon and the world that breaks faith. The dreadful irony of the poem is that though Keats locates blindness and failed emotion with Saturn as a Miltonic character, and purges emotion from his own style, that purgation makes the style the precursor's: as readers agree, *Hyperion* is one of the most perfect Miltonic poems since Milton. Keats has attempted the objective calm, the absence of subjective emotion and lyricism of the epic; but the sovereign who rules the poem is Milton, as Keats's development briefly digresses from authentic confrontation.

4

Where the Daemon Is

> The books say that our happiness comes from the opposite of hate. . . . And plainly, when I have closed a book too stirred to go on reading, and in those brief intense visions of sleep, I have something about me that, though it makes me love, is more like innocence. I am in the place where the daemon is.
>
> Yeats, *Per Amica Silentia Lunae*

In *Sunday Morning,* a poem that meditates the need for "The holy hush of ancient sacrifice," Wallace Stevens questions the destructive power of his chief character's idea of otherness: "Why should she give her bounty to the dead?" he muses. The question reflects the poet's effort to resist self-surrender, the submission that seems necessary to lyrical voice. Part of Stevens's great humanizing effort is directed toward securing our existence from the diminution effected by the idea of sublimity, which includes "the dead" who are the past, those parental figures whose physical deaths scarcely preclude their continued life in the mind. Throwing off this burden of the past, and discovering a present moment that is the origin of a self that is wholly free from otherness, is thus both a naive and genuinely compelling wish. The idealized other is imperishable, and so must be approached, even with loss, if any true freedom is to be won. On the other hand, some of our finest poems, such as Keats's *Ode to Psyche,* partly resist the necessary (if "ancient") sacrifice of full confrontation, in the apparent hope that the daemon of otherness is sympathetic rather than antithetical, and that the poet therefore can enter a life-giving relationship without

conceding the necessity of sorrow. The grand fiction of emotional existence is that the place of the daemon is the scene
of innocence, that the poet can have gain without loss.

Quotations from two contemporary literary theorists indicate the complex give-and-take of the relation of the poet
to otherness. Geoffrey Hartman, in an analysis of lyricism
that I cited earlier, considers the problem of the "confrontation of person with shadow or self with self": "The intense
lyricism of the Romantics," he concludes, "may well be related to this confrontation. For the Romantic 'I' emerges
nostalgically when certainty and simplicity of self are lost. In
a lyric poem it is clearly not the first-person form that moves
us (the poem need not be in the first person) but rather the I
toward which that I reaches." My second citation, though it
describes a prior element in the confrontation, comes from
Harold Bloom: "The poet of any guilt culture whatsoever,"
according to Bloom, "is compelled to accept a lack of priority
in creation. . . ." Consequently, his relationship to the muse
becomes tainted with ambivalence. "He has come late in the
story, but she has always been central in it, and he rightly
fears that his impending catastrophe is only another in her
litany of sorrows. What is his sincerity to her?" [2]

Keats's poetic development yokes together both the fear
that Bloom writes of and the reaching out of the "I" toward
the other that Hartman perceives, and, as I think, the reaching is done *despite* the poet's melancholy awareness that the
other is as much a principle of death as of antithetical life.
There is a dual significance to this reaching. First, it is in the
reaching that the poet transcends Freud's elemental narcissism, which is one of the most withering charges to poetry
and one of the most difficult to refute. The poet's reaching
out is neither an attempt only to seduce the id nor an attempt only to satisfy the strictures of an ego ideal: it is an instance of what Yeats in the description of the beams of the
cross calls the "nobleness of the arts," and it is at such moments that the poet achieves what Hartman refers to as an
"intense lyricism." It is also during these moments that the
poet is able to turn from the past to the future, from nos-

talgia to destiny, and can give up the "remembrance" that
Keats, for one, found so difficult to relinquish. In a very
powerful insight that is congruent with Freud's understanding, Yeats, remembering that Heraclitus claimed that
"the Daemon is our destiny," derives this ambivalent concept
of personal destiny: "When I think of life as a struggle with
the Daemon who would ever set us to the hardest work
among those not impossible, I understand why there is a
deep enmity between a man and his destiny, and why a man
loves nothing but his destiny." [3] The poet's turn to the daemon is a turn from the instinctual richness of the past to his
own antithetical destiny, his own future, and when he consciously embraces the daemon he does so with the awareness
that it is the daemon who has broken him, and who yet must
be loved. To love only the daemon is to renounce the
fullness of past emotional life; conversely, any self-sufficiency not based upon a relation to the other is to dally
with an imaginative surmise that retains the past but that
may be false. To concede the power of the other yet still to
affirm emotional life—this is to both perceive and feel, to
"See better," as Kent advises Lear, yet to accept with love the
self's lack of complete self-sufficiency.

This I think is an accurate formula, but poets, fortunately,
tend not to be formulaic. Keats, like Stevens, suggests the
difficulty of a renunciation that gives over one's bounty to
the dead. Even after hitting upon sorrow as both a new and
valid element of poetic experience and a way of diminishing
the threat of the sublime, Keats in the great odes and in *The
Fall of Hyperion* tends to resist the summons to dialogue and
its necessary concessions. Even the more antithetical Yeats,
we recall, at times sought the place where body is not
bruised to pleasure soul. For Yeats the encounter with the
other finally becomes a matter of forgiveness, which the
poet, having given power to the daemon, finds it necessary
to seek. Keats's quest in the revised *Hyperion* is partly based
upon his desire to prove himself worthy, a prior condition of
self-forgiveness. But Keats I think both more strongly resists
the daemon and more broadly humanizes it than Yeats does,

and it is this bimodal approach that characterizes the mature poems.

IDENTIFICATION AND IDENTITY: THE "ODE TO PSYCHE" AND THE "ODE TO A NIGHTINGALE"

Keats was rather pleased with the *Ode to Psyche,* the first of the odes he composed in the spring of 1819. But the ode has defied most of our attempts to define its greatness, much as we may sense it. Bate summarizes the problems for the reader: "It is justly felt that the ode may be something of a prototype for the others that follow it within the next month—that Keats was trying to do something in this first ode that he develops or redirects in the later ones. But, finding the poem so elusive, we return to it only after we know the others far better. If we had hoped to use them as keys, we discover they do not quite fit the lock. Meanwhile they have given us a standard hard to equal. Hence we either feel a disappointment about the 'Ode to Psyche' or else, remembering the care Keats supposedly gave it, we once more put the poem aside for future consideration." [4]

Bate's analysis is quite cogent, but I think we err to approach the poem from the perspective of the other odes, which are, as I shall suggest, of another order. A more satisfying approach can be found through the earlier poems, especially—though the forms are so different—*Hyperion,* which has as one of its major themes the loss inherent in love. Keats, with his wonderfully empathic nature, his ready ability to go out of self, must have taken to heart the tragedy of Saturn, whose divine freedom is wrested from him essentially because he eased his heart in love. That unfortunate submission calls forth a tendency to objectivity that is uncharacteristic of Keats. The *Ode to Psyche* returns to the problem of love, but with two important differences: the poet attempts to secure self-possession before opening the self to love; and the scene of the encounter with otherness becomes radically internalized as a result of his efforts to avoid the "pathetic" fate of Saturn and Clymene.

These at least seem to be among the intentions of the poem, or two of the factors that motivate it. But there is a complication involved in this general scheme that helps to account for the difference, which Bate points out, between this ode and the other great odes. I have discussed *Hyperion* in terms of the difficulty the poet or any man faces in accepting the diminution caused by the necessary presence of sorrow. What redeems the acceptance is that it frees the self from a commitment to hatred, as Yeats says, or ambivalence, in Freud's term, and so makes possible a modicum of self-acceptance. But it is diminishing, nevertheless, and is more easily evaded than faced. The *Ode to Psyche* is a response to the kind of loss depicted in *Hyperion,* but it follows the path of internalization rather than confrontation, and though the poem beautifully attempts a fusion of self-possession and a capacity for love, the results are problematic (to analysis, as opposed to enjoyment) and suggest a distinction between this and the forthcoming odes.

After an invocation to Psyche that should be read in terms of the conclusion of the poem, and to which we therefore shall return, the poet begins the first movement proper, which centers on his discovery of the goddess in the company of Love:

> Surely I dreamt to-day, or did I see
> The wingèd Psyche with awakened eyes?
> I wandered in a forest thoughtlessly,
> And, on the sudden, fainting with surprise,
> Saw two fair creatures, couchèd side by side.

Proceeding from his characteristic opposition between sleep or dream and a more truthful mode, the poet makes "awakened" both literal and metaphoric: have his eyes, those eyes that faced blindness in earlier poems as a result of contact with the sublime, crossed the threshold into true vision? Let us consider that possibility. The "forest" in which the poet "wandered" is, as is usually the case in Keats, the forest of romance, the place where one can exist "thoughtlessly," because its existence predates or is of another dimension

from that of the thinking principle. "Wandering" therefore
retains some of its Miltonic association with error. If the poet
indeed was dreaming, we infer, then this was merely the
romance world that satisfies in a nonintellectual way. But if
his eyes have been awakened, then the landscape becomes
something more than this, a place of possibility that was lost
to literal vision.

There are, quite obviously, two opposed assertions in the
initial statement, the first made in a confident declarative
("Surely I . . .") that does not survive the interrogative that
is the second. The resulting two-edged possibility carries
over into the next lines as well, in which the poet's wandering is intercepted by his "fainting with surprise." Surprise, as
we know from *Hyperion,* suggests an unexpected (if hoped
for) return: without prior familiarity there could be no recognition, and hence no surprise. Thus we have here, as well
as in the fragmentary epic, an association between surprise
and return or renewal, as Saturn sought beautiful things for
the "surprise" of the fallen Titans. In the ode, the surprise
brings on the poet's "fainting." As readers have observed,
fainting or swooning are favorite devices in Keats, and
usually augur the onset of vision. This is not quite what
occurs here: what seems to be taking place in this poem with
which Keats (as he wrote to the George Keatses) for the first
time took "moderate pains," is a recapitulation of an earlier
mode, in which Endymion gave his eyes to death when he
encountered Cynthia, only to learn that he began to live
more richly. "Fainting with surprise" thus suggests the
beneficence of return, and what is returned in the ode is the
possibility of love, represented by the "two fair creatures" in
the grass. They are, as we will learn, Cupid and Psyche; but
they are also Adam and Eve, who are the "two fair Creatures" of *Paradise Lost,*[5] and whose presence implies the innocence implicit in the return.

The importance of returns is hard to overemphasize.
They ease a fear of loss, and so are restorative, as is sug-
gested by another echo in the image of the two lovers, in
Keats's early sonnet *When I Have Fears:*

> And when I feel, fair creature of an hour,
>   That I shall never look upon thee more,
> Never have relish in the fairy power
>   Of unreflecting love; then on the shore
> Of the wide world I stand alone and think
> Till love and fame to nothingness do sink.

I shall suggest, as we get further into the ode, a close relation between its content and a fear of loss of relationship, so
we do not need to fit the later text to the meaning of the
sonnet without regard for differences between them. We
may note, even so, that the "fairy power" of the love found
in the forest of romance depends upon continual presence
or return, and conversely, passes to a "nothingness" that the
poet also feared in *Sleep and Poetry* and *Endymion.* When his
fear of the departure of his fair creature becomes overwhelming, the poet subsumes his own belief in "love and
fame" to thought and, like the "pathetic" figures he annotates, retires to "the shore" of the world. This terrible purgation of the emotional self helps to explain Keats's repudiation of the Wordsworthian sublime. While on that shore, as
he says, "I stand alone," a solitary posture similar to that of
the "egotistical sublime," which is "a thing per se and stands
alone." [6] The sonnet sets the fairy power of "unreflecting
love" against the thoughts that master fear by emptying the
self of relationship.

It is partly against the rising of such antithetical thoughts
that the ode is written, as is implied in the hyperbolic pro-
trait of love in the forest:

> Their lips touched not, but had not bade adieu,
>   As if disjoinèd by soft-handed slumber,
>   And ready still past kisses to outnumber
>   At tender eye-dawn of aurorean love.

As Apollo was the figure of dawn in *Hyperion,* love in its
romance form is "aurorean" here, thereby heralding a
dawning of the eyes. These are the lovers that do not bid
adieu, for their minimal separation is lapped and lulled by

slumber, and they remain ready "still"—in the sense of "always"—to return to passion. The portrait of Cupid and Psyche thus reinvigorates not merely a belief in love, but a belief in the power of love to not be diminishing, as it was for Saturn. Now, having created such a possibility once more, the poet can identify his creatures: "The wingèd boy I knew; / But who wast thou, O happy, happy dove? / His Psyche true!" Of course he knows the boy: it is, as we will learn, himself. The more important discovery is of Psyche and of her "true" nature, by which she obviates fears of separation.

The first movement of the poem ends with the return or rebirth of romance, then, which tends to be Spenserian in Keats. The romance world is the scene of a beauty the poet finds it difficult to give up, despite the pressing sense that there *are* no returns, for it is the scene in which otherness is made loving. That sounds high-handed and may suggest to readers the dangerous significations of the concept of the primal scene, yet I think the assertion is supported by the poem. In the early and frankly non-mythic poem *Woman! When I Behold Thee Flippant, Vain,* Keats, as we have seen, assumes a chivalric role in the hope that he might "be loved by thee like these of yore." There is humor in those early lines, but there is also a true wish for the beneficence of relationship—a relationship that depends upon the poet's acting as the "defender" of a "meek" and "tender" woman. The *Ode to Psyche* also enacts a subtle chivalry, in which the scene and the figure of encounter are defended by an internalization that completes the desire to be loved and makes loving possible. At the same time, internalization becomes a means of retaining self, and thereby protecting the poet against diminution, since the relationship with otherness now becomes subjective.

As the potentially beneficent muse who appears to need the sanctuary of the poet's love, Psyche is suitably described as the fairest but most unappreciated flower in the landscape of divinity. My allusion to Milton's reference to Eve as the "fairest unsupported Flow'r, / From her best prop so far"

(IX, 432–33) claims too much; but there is something in Keats's description of Psyche that is both Eve-ish and reminiscent of the "fair creature of an hour":

> O latest born and loveliest vision far
>> Of all Olympus' faded hierarchy!
> Fairer than Phoebe's sapphire-regioned star,
>> Or Vesper, amorous glow-worm of the sky;
> Fairer than these, though temple thou hast none,
>> Nor altar heaped with flowers;
> Nor virgin-choir to make delicious moan
>> Upon the midnight hours—
> No voice, no lute, no pipe, no incense sweet
>> From chain-swung censer teeming;
> No shrine, no grove, no oracle, no heat
>> Of pale-mouthed prophet dreaming.

Psyche's lateness places her in need of a devotee, and Keats from the first was attracted to the romance of meek womanhood. She of course has allegorical significance as well, and in this capacity her need is also understandable. And, as well as being the last born, she is the "loveliest," and so manifests a way by which loveliness can be retained, even if different in kind from that of earlier times:

> O brightest, though too late for antique vows!
>> Too, too late for the fond believing lyre,
> When holy were the haunted forest boughs,
>> Holy the air, the water and the fire.
> Yet even in these days so far retired
>> From happy pieties, thy lucent fans,
>> Fluttering among the faint Olympians,
> I see, and sing, by my own eyes inspired.

There is a double movement in this passage, from past to present and from outer to inner. The poet's address to the "brightest," leaves marvelously ambiguous the objective-subjective identity of his auditor, for this is both the muse and the mind that conceives her. With "though," we begin a compelling movement *away* from the past and from outer

glory, even as these are being discussed. As the poet laments
the passing of these, he nevertheless has been arrested by
the brightness he senses, and so moves naturally to the positive alternative of "Yet" and contemporary consolation.
What follows is one of the most important statements Keats
has written thus far, a proclamation of the poet's necessary
blindness to outer things. This recognition, so movingly resisted in earlier poems and coupled there with loss of voice,
here becomes a victory—though with some qualifica-
tions—over both the past and the world that disappoints in
its inability to harbor loveliness. One thinks of Keats turning
his eye away in a number of instances we have discussed,
and one turns oneself with pleasure to this seeing and to its
rightful and perhaps causative connection to creativity: "I
see, *and* sing."

The problem of romance is partly resolved in this culminating line, which (though it does not quite conclude the
second movement) prepares us for the internalization described in the third movement of the poem. Keats has rescued the *goal* of romance quests without being impeded by
the notion of return which is central to its mode. Beautiful
things, such as the myths of the old Olympians, cannot be
made new, but the last vision is of the mind, and inward
sight can rescue the object of love, even if that object is now
tinged with a necessary ambivalence:

> Yes, I will be thy priest, and build a fane
> In some untrodden region of my mind,
> Where branchèd thoughts, new grown with pleasant pain,
> Instead of pines shall murmur in the wind.

The self-sufficiency of "by my own eyes inspired" grows to
self-acceptance in the oxymoronic "pleasant pain" of the
thoughts that replace the pines of the forest, in which the
poet wandered "thoughtlessly" in the first movement. The
old "lyre" of the ancients, and perhaps also the poet's early
verse, was "fond" in the sense of "foolish"—Cupid and
Psyche do not come to surprise the poet unless his eyes are
awakened to themselves. There is pain in internalization, for

it follows the separation or loss of outer objects described in the second movement; but there is pleasure as well, as the mind is made capable of retaining what it seeks, and has sought. "Yes" is therefore an affirmation of devotion to a muse that corresponds to a portion of the self, though there is also loss (of the pines) in "Instead." The daemon, as Yeats says, leads the poet to the place of choice and insists upon sacrifice as a means to fulfillment. Oceanus, we recall, thought that "truth" should cause no "pain" to those who had achieved sovereignty. The partiality of his view, and the rightfulness of the apparent self-contradiction of the oxymoron, is evident in Keats's "pleasant pain."

The old romance, both as form and as a fiction that makes life possible, is now laid to rest with the dryads of the landscape of the mind: "And there by zephyrs, streams, and birds, and bees, / The moss-lain Dryads shall be lulled to sleep." Early loveliness sleeps, and with it, return; but the poet with awakened eyes creates an alternative—a continual newness that satisfies the mind's need for discontinuity and so provides a proper scene for love:

> And in the midst of this wide quietness
> A rosy sanctuary will I dress
> With the wreathed trellis of a working brain,
>   With buds, and bells, and stars without a name,
> With all the gardener Fancy e'er could feign,
>   Who breeding flowers will never breed the same:
> And there shall be for thee all soft delight
>   That shadowy thought can win,
> A bright torch, and a casement ope at night,
>   To let the warm Love in!

This magnificent conclusion details an increasing internalization, a progressive withdrawal from all that is outside the mind, until "delight"—even the perhaps melancholy delight of shadowy thought—is found once more. By the subtlest of circumambulations, we realize that we have been brought to the scene we thought we had left (in the first stanza, as well as in previous romances), but with a difference, with the newness dispensed by the Fancy, who never stops creating, but whose creations abandon repetition for change. Hyperion, caught by his own growing awareness of life as a series of linear moments, desperately wanted to begin the day early, to make a dawn out of darkness, "if but for change." Though a primeval god, he could not do so, for the sacred seasons, as Keats writes, could not be disturbed. But change comes to the topography of the last stanza of the ode as "new" thoughts, and as the absence of sameness in the flowers that soften that wonderfully ambivalent region.

There is a suspension of the willful self here, as naming is resisted—Apollo in his transformation had learned "Names" as part of his "Knowledge enormous" (III, 114)—and there is darkness in the clustered trees and shadowy thought. And there is the nobleness of surrender in the casement that is left open to Love, despite the seeming necessity of withdrawal. This is so thoroughly Keatsean that we can hardly distinguish identities in the last lines: is the figure of Love Keats as well as Cupid, entering the sanctuary of the muse as well as Psyche? Or is it the sanctuary of mind that belongs to the poet, in which he maintains an openness to a love that is external? One hardly asks these questions of the projected embrace, so compelling is the sense of wholeness that the last line, especially, achieves. We are on enchanted ground, won by surrender and self-retention.

If we regretfully terminate our own surrender to the image, however, we may contrast the ambiguous figure at the end with the goddess the poet addresses at the opening of the poem: "O Goddess! Hear these tuneless numbers, wrung / By sweet enforcement and remembrance dear, / And pardon that thy secrets should be sung / Even into thine own soft-conchèd ear." The poet already has fashioned relationship in terms of oxymoron, we note—"sweet enforcement" and "remembrance dear," where "dear," as in Spenser and *Lycidas* (1. 6), indicates both cherished and costly. Of what does the remembrance consist? On the basis of the poem, one would say perhaps that it consists of the encounter in the forest, which follows upon the invocation. But

in this poem about earlier pieties, which includes glancing
allusions to the poet's previous poetry, that remembrance
may pertain to the subject of lines such as these, from the
sonnet *To* ——— ("Had I a man's fair form"), written in Feb-
ruary, 1816:

> Had I a man's fair form, then might my sighs
>   Be echoed swiftly through that ivory shell
>   Thine ear, and find thy gentle heart, so well
> Would passion arm me for the enterprise.

By the time he writes the ode, Keats is armed for the enterprise with a knowledge of Psyche's "secrets," and the ability to effect chivalric conquest by means of internalization:
after all, even in the last stanza, the poet promises his
goddess all the delight that shadowy thought can "win." "Remembrance dear" in the ode may well involve a memory of
Psyche as the goddess who has always been the object of the
poet's romantic quest, at least in a certain mode of his poetry.

That mode is not one we ordinarily recognize as comprising a separate category, but it centers on the appearance of
the benignant (rather than threatening or fearful) muse and
stems from the Miltonic poems of the eighteenth century. A
number of elements of our conceptual apparatus dovetail
here. The tendency of the mind to *retain* relationships,
which we earlier associated with Yeats's "emotional" mode of
poetry, is the background to the device of the "return," the
situation in which what has been lost is found again. The *Ode
to Psyche,* though a poem we are used to talking about in
terms of "imagination," is more understandable as a poem of
return, where the return is sublimated and effected by internalization. The exclusiveness of that internalization,
which seems to shut out the "real world," has disturbed a
number of readers, and I would like at this point to call up
as from the vasty deep some of our psychological concepts,
however cumbersome these may appear next to the delicate
modulations of Keats's ode.

We began with a consideration of Saturn's unfortunate

love, which I think is a proper prelude to the ode. Saturn, whose dilemma is characterized by the literary term "pathos" (a favorite of Hazlitt's and frequent in Keats's various annotations), suffers a catastrophic object-loss. As I mentioned in the Preface, terminology is a problem, for Freud's effort to translate emotion to the more acceptable vocabulary of science deprives the experience he describes of some of its value for us. Object-loss is the "disappointment" in the world that Yeats believes creates the antithetical poet and seems to confirm a dark suspicion that he has nothing. The *Ode to Psyche* is not an antithetical poem, but it does represent a response to object-loss. When the poet lovingly complains about the "tuneless numbers" being "wrung" from him by "sweet enforcement" and "remembrance dear," he is recollecting a time before loss: his remembrance straddles his loss of Psyche, and therefore is "dear" to him. The exuberance of the opening lines of the poem seems to be the result of his feeling that he has found her again and can re-establish a tie to her, though now she must be Psyche rather than Cynthia or Phoebe: she is "Fairer than these" because she is accessible once again, though only in the sphere of the mind.

In the beginning was narcissism, as the gospel of Freud tells us. Narcissism undergoes some modification as a result of object-choice (our "relationship"), which is inevitable, and which proceeds from the id, "which feels erotic trends as needs." An object-choice expresses the desire to possess the object, to bring it into the mind. Alternatively, early experience may consist of "identification," in which the mind assumes the qualities of the object by imitating it rather than possessing it: it is this dynamic that informs Freud's extraordinary rendering of the ego's words to the id: "Look, you can love me too—I am so like the object." [7] When an object is lost—that is, when a loved person or thing is no longer available to the mind—it may respond in any of several ways: the mind may choose another object; it may withdraw the energy expended on the other into itself in some unspecified way; or, it may "establish an *identification* of the ego with the abandoned object." [8] The mind thus introjects, or internalizes, what had been lost, though it has had to do so by giving up the object in favor of a subjective representation of it. What had been outer is now inner, and though a kind of reality is given up, a new satisfaction accrues from the return. "The transformation of object-libido into narcissistic libido," in Freud's terms, also represents "a kind of sublimation"—in fact, perhaps the only kind.[9]

The concluding movement of Keats's ode follows much of this general pattern. The early object of his chivalric quest returns as the psyche itself, thus transforming an object-loss like Saturn's into a compensatory internalization. The mind discovers that it can love without fear of loss, but the nobleness of this victory is tempered at first by the subjectivity involved, and the victory itself becomes a partial narcissism. I do not think, however, that this "explains" the entirety of the last stanza. The last two lines allude to a projected sexual embrace, and though it is true that the last word of the poem culminates this union, the "open casement" maintains relationship to the mind's idea of otherness as external. This suggestion in the lines reintroduces the possible vulnerability of the mind by making it subject to a reality seen to be external, and by so doing converts an identification to an object-choice once again. The mode of the *Ode to Psyche* is that of sublimation, but Keats transcends the mode and at the same time recreates a relationship to outer things.

The openness at the conclusion of the *Ode to Psyche* thus goes beyond internalization and sublimation, though its mode is characterized by these. Internalizations that follow outer loss are compensatory and reflect a desire to restore what is lost by a repetition in a finer tone of what has gone. Freud tells us that "Identification is known to psychoanalysis as the earliest expression of an *emotional* tie with another person." [10] The process of internalization by identification after loss is a means of re-establishing that emotional tie, and this is one way by which we can understand the various returns of what I, following Yeats, have called "emotional" poetry. (By this I do not mean poetry that has emotion, of course, but poetry that seeks the return of a previous relationship.) Thus, for instance, Joseph Warton's wish for "Fancy" to "remove" the "pangs of absence" is self-compensatory, as we noted in the first chapter. We now can see in that compensation a somewhat crude form of identification, in which Fancy "canst place me near my love" as his love is translated to subjective form, and his "visionary bliss" assumes the features of a renewed narcissistic relationship.

The antithetical strain in poetry, which from the outset has appeared qualitatively different from "emotional" poems, represents an antithesis to emotional loss, in this sense: the mind confronts not a subjective representation (or re-representation) of a lost object but an ideal that is no longer part of an emotional relationship. That is, the antithetical is to be distinguished from the sublimation of a previous object-choice. Instead, the poet must satisfy the antithetical as an ideal imposed upon the mind, which accepts it as an ideal. Identifications are internalizations that "surprise" the poet by restoring a lost relationship—say, to a Keatsean "loveliness." The antithetical manifests itself as an ego ideal which makes a demand upon him which can only be met in some fashion—but it is not internalized, except as it is seen to have been internalized by an earlier poet, who then becomes associated with it. Thus antithetical broodings imply parental presence, as the ego ideal takes on the features of a succession of parental figures. It is difficult to avoid noting the connection between the sublime and the parent, though the question of the relation of epiphany to parental presence is one to which we shall return.

Whereas the *Ode to Psyche* is a poem in the emotional mode (though without the natural component, since we are now dealing with internalization), the *Ode to a Nightingale* portrays ✱ an encounter with an ideal that is antithetical to emotional ties. The famous opening of the ode describes not the initial moment of encounter but a time after the encounter has begun. This is an important distinction, because as we read the first line, the poet has *already* lost self to the seeming demands of the other and so is very much in the same pre-

dicament as Saturn at the opening of *Hyperion,* or as Clymene, who experiences a "living death" as a consequence of
hearing a "blissful golden melody." The bird's song similarly
begins to deprive the poet of life—the life of the "heart" and
the "sense," for these elements of relationship are threatened by the poet's transferring his love to that singer in the
trees:

> My heart aches, and a drowsy numbness pains
>   My sense, as though of hemlock I had drunk,
> Or emptied some dull opiate to the drains
>   One minute past, and Lethe-wards had sunk.
> 'Tis not through envy of thy happy lot,
>   But being too happy in thine happiness—
>   That thou, light-wingèd Dryad of the trees,
>   In some melodious plot
>   Of beechen green, and shadows numberless,
>   Singest of summer in full-throated ease.

The poet's "being too happy" in the bird's own happiness is
an instance of "the feel" of feeling—though, as is usual in
Keatsean encounters, there is a cost to him in the exercise of
such empathy. As love for the antithetical other—a love that
is self-surrender—increases, the emotional self is diminished. This threatened loss of self is one way in which the
nightingale cheats the poet: it cannot be internalized, the
way Psyche was, and by maintaining its remove and demand-
ing the poet's love, it brings about the dangerous feelings of
the first two lines. The bird's "ease" is thus ironically recalled
in the "easeful Death" the poet invokes later in the poem.

In this context, and with an eye toward Keats's marvelous
ability to pun tellingly, the "melodious plot" seems also a
"plot" against the poet, an intentional policy of deception.
Regardless of these possible threatening elements, however,
the poet responds with sympathetic happiness and a delight
in the nightingale's ability to sing of the fullness of summer,
which is still in the offing. The bird sings of a future fulfillment: the poet, as we learn, cannot "forget" the misery of
past and present. The basis of the conflict is, then, largely es-

tablished in this opening stanza. The nightingale's song has come melodiously to the poet's ear, as the voice of love sounded "melodious" to the Indian Maiden in *Endymion,* and like the sorrowful Maiden the poet is threatened with self-diminution. Keats does not resist, for to do so would be to affirm the egotistical sublime that stands alone. Keats casts out "envy" in favor of a form of negative capability in which he allows the high strains to play upon his sensibility. The soul, as he wrote in his journal letter to the George Keatses, is created by the action of the world on the heart.[11]

At this point, we usually think of the rest of the poem as a successful attempt to join the nightingale, followed by the poet's inevitable separation from it. I myself find that joining ambiguous, and in any case I think there is a more important motive that develops from the encounter: the poet is "caught" by the song at the outset, but as the poem progresses he affirms not the antithetical but the emotional, not the music of heaven but the poetry of earth. An extraordinary generosity may be glimpsed in the poem, as the poet sacrifices self to otherness in what increasingly looks like an attempt to humanize that otherness, by providing it with an emotional context it in itself lacks. In the *Ode to a Nightingale* we begin to reach a more balanced relationship between poet and muse, in which the poet gives even as he begins to understand that the bird does not, except by its presence.

The second stanza invokes wine as a means of reaching the bird and leaving the world "unseen" in its company. That attempt, as readers know, is unsuccessful: it is not until the fourth stanza that the poet learns that the "viewless wings of Poesy," by a sort of fiat, are the only way to the nightingale. It does not seem, however, as if the second stanza—there are only eight in the poem—could be devoted to a mere error of approach. Rather, the wine that the speaker turns to represents an antithesis to the bird—he is even at this point momentarily drawing back from it, in an affirmation of the values that he will later affirm. There is nothing that suggests ecstasy in the wine, which might indeed advance the poet's cause, if this were merely to achieve union with a sublime other. This is a "vintage," as the poet refers to it, that tastes "Of Flora and the country green," and "that hath been / Cooled a long age in the deep-delvèd earth." That is, this is the wine of romance (Flora) rather than the sublime, and if sacramental at all it is so of the earth, not the sky. "Deep-delvèd" suggests the cultivation of the soil, and the cellars used for aging Keats's favorite wine, claret. But it suggests too the ritual of burial, of continual burials and of generations gone before, all of them into that earthly resting place. As such, the image anticipates both the "valley-glades" in which the bird's song is "buried deep" at the end of the poem, and the later toast to mortality that the poet makes in *The Fall of Hyperion.* And it implies an alternative sphere to that of the nightingale, whose presence is necessary to make the ground enchanted, but who has never been part of the human story, of the pathos that Keats has chosen as a necessary basis for imaginative speculation. The second stanza, then, at the same time that it searches for access to the nightingale, delights in the earthly pleasures of wine and romance, and a sensual bliss of which the bird is not a part:

> Oh, for a beaker full of the warm South,
>   Full of the true, the blushful Hippocrene,
>   With beaded bubbles winking at the brim,
>   And purple-stainèd mouth,
>   That I might drink, and leave the world unseen,
>   And with thee fade away into the forest dim.

The poet, in a way, is still sparring, in a somewhat Hamlet-like fashion: he has been summoned and has pledged a portion of his allegiance, but he has yet to expose himself to the pain of transition.

The problem is that to join the bird is indeed to "leave the world unseen"—in the double sense, perhaps, of not seeing it as well as not being seen—and so to lose the portraiture intense that remembrance stores. Yet Keats has already ascertained (in earlier poems) the impossibility of recalling romance. He must, then, join the bird, though retain self in doing so. This dilemma informs the third stanza, which describes the close correlation between "forgetting" human existence and murdering the self that remembers:

> Fade far away, dissolve, and quite forget
> What thou among the leaves hast never known.

The nightingale sings in the dim forest. But to know suffering is also to dim the eyes, though in a contrary way. The "Here" that is earth is a place

> Where but to think is to be full of sorrow
> And leaden-eyed despairs;
> Where Beauty cannot keep her lustrous eyes,
> Or new Love pine at them beyond to-morrow.

The sorrow of thought—which Gray believes destroys paradise—both dims the luster of the eyes and freezes them in despair. This is the burden of pathos, which sees and knows only fleetingness: all its knowledge is that joy is gone. Where in the *Ode to Psyche* Keats replaced literal pines with thought, he here finds even emotional pining of brief duration. "As / The physical pine, the metaphysical pine," as Stevens writes in *Credences of Summer*.

The graphic despair of the stanza almost seems a necessary prelude to the declaration by which the poet finally launches himself into the vicinity of the nightingale. The reminders of palsy and the premature death of youth evoke a reflexive desire to leave that world. "Away! away!" the poet calls to the bird and vows to join it despite the tendency of the mind to find ambivalence in experience—"Though the dull brain perplexes and retards." The wings of Poesy carry the poet to the region of bird and moon, who perhaps ("haply") overlooks this sacrificial loss of the world from her throne in the night sky:

> Already with thee! Tender is the night,
> And haply the Queen-Moon is on her throne,
> Clustered around by all her starry fays;
> But here there is no light.

" 'Twas to live," Endymion found when he submitted to otherness. That quality of reward is present in these lines as well, though it is as much a reward that the poet bestows as receives. From the outset he softens the darkness: "Tender is the night" is already the beginning of oxymoron, of an antiphonal music of which the nightingale's is only one strain. We note that even the presence of the moon is a surmise, for there is no light "here" where the poet is. Whether the poet is indeed "with" the bird is therefore somewhat debatable. In the next stanza we discover him in the forest, yes, but with his feet on the ground. And if the bird is meant to bring him to the saving light of the moon—Cynthia enthroned—it clearly fails to do so.

With the light gone and the light of visual sense gone out, Keats, in one of his most magnificent passages, nevertheless suspends irritable reaching out in favor of allowing the burden of the mystery to assert itself. The result is a mingling of presence and absence that is unmatched, for the flowers that grow in this landscape recall but are different from those that fill the forests of romance:

> I cannot see what flowers are at my feet,
>   Nor what soft incense hangs upon the boughs,
> But in embalmèd darkness, guess each sweet
>   Wherewith the seasonable month endows
> The grass, the thicket, and the fruit-tree wild—
>   White hawthorn, and the pastoral eglantine;
>   Fast-fading violets covered up in leaves.

The poet, necessarily, cannot see; but his dark grows luminous and fruitful. Keats is remembering the flowers of *A Midsummer Night's Dream* (II, i, 249–52) and perhaps also those of *Lycidas* (ll.142–48), but those flowers survive mortality: when Edward King is gone they adopt their "sad embroidery," but the landscapes of both works exist out of time. Keats's flowers know death, know mutability, and never grew in any other landscape.

Thus there are echoes here of other poets and other poems, but the stanza could have been written only by Keats.

Wordsworth, in also taking up the burden of the mystery, looked downward to "The Pansy at my feet" (The *Intimations* ode, 1. 54). Keats again refuses to name, at the outset, though knowledge comes: "I cannot see what flowers are at my feet." This is mortal enchantment, a fire that is only earthly, yet it arises from two elements, each equally necessary. With the flowers, Keats summons, as it were, his ghostly poetic fathers—Shakespeare, Milton, Wordsworth. Their pastoral was his original poetic region and recurs in the early poems in *1817*. That summons is made inevitable by the presence of the nightingale, the reminder of Milton, especially: this is the positive side of poetic influence, for fatheral (or parental) presence is necessary to the sublime of the sublime pathetic, to negative capability, as well as to the earlier sublime ode. The second element is the combination of self-acceptance and love, or inner and outer sympathy, that allows the flowers their mortality. There is no hint of "envy," no renunciation that would idealize the flowers and thereby freeze them into permanence. There is only the fullest and most compelling negative capability. The poet is neither the nightingale nor the Queen-Moon, but whereas Hyperion lamented that "I cannot see—but darkness, death and darkness," Keats here finds an "embalmèd darkness," an oxymoron that suggests both death and rich distilled perfume, of his own making. For this simultaneous concession and victory, in which he surrenders to his poetic fathers and yet retains his own feelingful vision, the poet is rewarded with a possible future, in which he, as poetic "child," comes into his own identity and appropriates to himself a "wine" that is not an old romance, and a "summer" that is his and not the nightingale's:

> And mid-May's eldest child,
> The coming musk-rose, full of dewy wine,
> The murmurous haunt of flies on summer eves.

If, as Freud came to believe, "character" is a precipitate of lost objects, each of which leaves its shadow on the ego, then this vision is the furthest reach of what it means to live in a

world where men grow spectre-thin and die, and even "new"
Love flickers in the coming darkness. The poet, who is so
powerfully drawn to pathetic representations, forgives their
transience as well as his own, and by this gives the darkness
its various perfumes. This capability in Keats is not unique
to him, but it is extraordinary and touches the other odes as
well. The poet has learned Psyche's "secrets" and knows that
beautiful things are not joys forever, and that the power of
otherness, which instills a fear for sight and for life, cannot
be resisted. Yet his feeling for vulnerable objects is so intense
as to almost redeem them, usually by means of an adjective
that implies both that vulnerability and sympathy—as in
these lines from the *Ode on a Grecian Urn:*

> Who are these coming to the sacrifice?
>   To what green altar, O mysterious priest,
> Lead'st thou that heifer lowing at the skies,
>   And all her silken flanks with garlands dressed?
> What little town by river or sea shore,
>   Or mountain-built with peaceful citadel,
>   Is emptied of this folk, this pious morn?
> And, little town, thy streets for evermore
>   Will silent be; and not a soul to tell
>   Why thou art desolate can e'er return.

"Little town": it is this recognition that terminates Keats's
empathic involvement in the life of the Grecian urn. The
poet cannot heal the desolation of the town any more than
he can return Orpheus to Calliope or Posthumus to Imogen.
But he gives it the gift of feeling, a modicum of recompense
for its fall into silence. The "sacrifice," presided over by a
"priest" of the mystery, has a quality of inevitability and
seems involuntary. The heifer, the town, and perhaps the
poet are caught in that mystery and that sacrifice and receive
redemption only from the poet. I find the same fair attitude
at work in the ode *To Autumn,* in which the fiction that
"Warm days will never cease" is maintained despite the
poet's awareness of a conspiracy behind the fiction. They are
still "Warm" days, and to give them this beneficent adjective
is to obviate both a fearful sublime and a static pathos.

That poetic surrender is partly a wished-for surrender to death is an inescapable conclusion. But to resist this is to deny the human beauty of the catalogue of flowers that die and the paradoxical strength the poet assumes in the face of an antithetical other that was never a part of death yet is involved in the poet's submission to it. As the bird continues to sing, the poet's listening regard begins to assume a deathly quietude, and the nightingale itself emerges as the poetic father, Milton's "wakeful Bird" that "Sings darkling":

> Darkling, I listen; and, for many a time
>   I have been half in love with easeful Death,
> Called him soft names in many a musèd rhyme,
>   To take into the air my quiet breath;
> Now more than ever seems it rich to die,
>   To cease upon the midnight with no pain,
>   While thou art pouring forth thy soul abroad
>   In such an ecstasy!

If the presence of the spectral other overwhelms the poet—enough so that he can envision a death without "pain," without contraries—it does so only as a result of his own softening love. I do not think we can separate death from otherness here: when Keats retrospectively states that he "Called him soft names in many a musèd rhyme," one cannot help seeing the muse in "musèd." Rhymes to the muse bring about addresses to death. To that muse and to that death, Keats surrenders a portion of self (he is only "half in love," after all), but he does so in a humanizing gesture that makes death not an object of terror but something "easeful." That word, curiously, takes us back to *Sleep and Poetry* and *L'Allegro;* but rather than the "heart-easing things" of those poems, which did not involve a penseroso strain, the poet juxtaposes his *emotional* tie to the thought of death the nightingale instills, and so mitigates that daemonic threat.

I earlier mentioned the ambiguity of the poet's union with the nightingale: do we not rather see a dialogue of a kind, in which the fatheral nightingale summons the poet to an otherwhere or otherwise (the fairy stealing mid-May's eldest child, as it were), while the poet affirms that his proper place

is his English ground, the region of mortal beauty? "Life to
him," Keats wrote of Milton (to the George Keatses on September 21, 1819), "would be death to me": "Chatterton's language is entirely northern—I prefer the native music of it to
Milton's cut by feet I have but lately stood on my guard
against Milton. Life to him would be death to me." The dialogue is more inclusive than one between the language of
Chatterton and that of Milton. Keats, since the fourth book
of *Endymion,* had been seeking the "Muse of my native land,"
as Chatterton seemed to have found a "native music." This
trend reflects a journey homeward to self from the otherness
that includes (among other elements) the presence of Milton. It is not clear that there can be a native muse, which in
its true form would exclude both otherness and epiphany.
But Keats chooses the "here" where there is no light, the
darkling region that shadows mortality, which is not the
scene of Milton's "Life" but also is not imaginative death to
himself. In the encounter with the nightingale, the poet's acceptance of necessary death paradoxically makes him the
spokesman for life.

Consequently, when Keats goes on to admire the fact that
"Thou wast not born for death, immortal bird," the compli-
ment is also mildly pejorative and serves to distance the
nightingale from human experience. The balance between
admiration and reservation continues through the presentation of the early history of the song:

> The voice I hear this passing night was heard
>   In ancient days by emperor and clown:
> Perhaps the self-same song that found a path
>   Through the sad heart of Ruth, when, sick for home,
>   She stood in tears amid the alien corn;
>   The same that oft-times hath
>   Charmed magic casements, opening on the foam
>   Of perilous seas in fairy lands forlorn.

The song is eastern, Biblical, and finally the song of romance, of the magic portals that frame the perilous visions
of fairyland. Its relation to the pathos of Ruth, standing in

tears, is wonderfully uncertain. We assume she was consoled by it, but the poet does not quite say so. Can an unchanging ("self-same") song console one who is "sick for home," if this is her native home? Or, from another perspective, can the notion of continuity console those tied to a "passing night"?

The answer to these questions must be yes and no. One hopes this is balance rather than evasion. Keats suggests the negative part in his repetition of the word "forlorn" in the next stanza, in which the inaccessibility of those lands draws the poet away from the nightingale as well. Forlornness, after all, is the later poet's mode rather than the bird's, and once the circumstance of pathos is suggested the separation is begun. (It is also a "native" English word, descended from the Middle English *foreloren*.) So the poet is tolled back to his "sole self," complains about the cheating and deceiving of the fancy (which have been apparent for some time), and bids the nightingale a melancholy farewell:

> Adieu! adieu! Thy plaintive anthem fades
> Past the near meadows, over the still stream,
> Up the hill-side; and now 'tis buried deep
> In the next valley-glades:
> Was it a vision, or a waking dream?
> Fled is that music . . . Do I wake or sleep?

The "yes" of the answer is apparent when we consider the landscape the bird is leaving: this is the "hill-side" that we associate with vision in Keats, but "the still stream" returns us to Saturn's dismal prospect, in which "A stream went voiceless by." There is a suggestion, then, that the departure of the nightingale disenchants the landscape, and therefore we infer the necessary presence of the other to the poet's song, even if this be in mortal notes. When the poet buries the bird's song, he cannot tell sleep from wakefulness: Milton's nightingale, on the other hand, is the wakeful bird.

The question of whether there can be an ode without the motivating presence of a sublime other is an open and fascinating one. Geoffrey Hartman finds that presence necessary to the *Nightingale* and *Grecian Urn* odes but suggests that

To Autumn exemplifies the "demise of epiphanic forms." [12]
The question is given added importance by the richness of
scene in the later poem, *To Autumn*, because in the *Ode to a
Nightingale* it seems that the deathly dimension of the bird
contributes to the creation of the poet's dark paradise in the
fifth stanza. Has the necessity of presence been put aside in
To Autumn, and has the poet taken upon himself the power
to enrich? That indeed would be a native music. Or, in terms
of the scheme we have been using, has the oxymoron of encounter been circumvented, and the poet's vision become
that of both god and man? This is the first of the poem's
three stanzas:

> Season of mists and mellow fruitfulness
>   Close bosom friend of the maturing sun,
> Conspiring with him how to load and bless
>   With fruit the vines that round the thatch-eaves
>   run:
> To bend with apples the mossed cottage-trees,
>   And fill all fruit with ripeness to the core;
>   To swell the gourd, and plump the hazel shells
>   With a sweet kernel; to set budding more,
> And still more, later flowers for the bees,
> Until they think warm days will never cease,
>   For summer has o'er-brimmed their clammy
>   cells.

The poet knows that there is a conspiracy behind this richness, that the fullness is a fact of the landscape, but to the
observer it is a fiction based on the idea of summer, and so is
a myth of fulfillment. This is an extremely moving myth,
which deceives us, with the bees, into forgetting that warmth
ceases with summer days and that autumn has already come.
The seeming present is already a past, though the suspension of time in the stanza tends to satisfy us that we have
reached a moment of stasis.

Do we achieve this rich plenitude without a dialogue between self and other? Hartman suggests that "Nothing remains of the cultic distance between votary and personified

power: we have instead two such powers, autumn and sun. . . ." [13] I myself think the presence of this distance is greatly muted but distinct. One might see in the "maturing sun" (1. 2) a pun that re-establishes the earlier relationship of votary and power, in the familial form this often assumes in Keats. The poet is the son who is maturing, and it is this maturation that mutes but does not extinguish the relationship to the goddess, Autumn. Mutes because that maturation has closed a gap: the relationship comprehends not inspiration so much as the breathing together that is "Conspiring." Autumn is the goddess even before her personified appearance in the second stanza. She is the beneficent goddess that is a "friend" to man, as the poem reiterates in part the relation of the Grecian urn to the poet in that ode. As such, she suspends her tasks of harvesting in the second stanza. But it is clear there that she augurs death—however much it ripens life—and, in fact, always has. It is also clear, nevertheless, that the poet has learned to conspire with her, to do his own gleaning of a fullness that needs her for its definition, at the same time that she only acquires definition in his myth: when he asks "Who hath not seen thee?" he praises her in large measure for his own power, for the answer is that she lives only in the poet's eye.

The relation of poet to muse in *To Autumn* thus involves an interdependence, in which the destructive element of otherness is softened by an imagination that needs the presence of that other. The poem is more like the *Nightingale* ode than the muted presence of the poet at first indicates, though as Hartman says, the poet in *To Autumn* does not suffer disenchantment in the final stanza.[14] Nor is the lyricism of the later ode as intense. The "shady visions" that come to domineer in the *Nightingale* ode have a more powerful presence and evoke a darker response that is more directly felt by the poet: the sun has not yet matured this vision. By "felt" I mean felt as threat, and it is this that makes the response more intense.

Yet both poems reap the harvest of the presence of otherness. In his essay *On Gusto,* included in the *Round Table,* which Keats read with great admiration, Hazlitt complains that Claude Lorrain's landscapes suffered because the painter's "eye wanted imagination; it did not strongly sympathize with his other faculties. He saw the atmosphere, but he did not feel it." [15] Though in 1816 Keats thought the poet's eye differed from ordinary vision in its ability to see further, he learns that the poet actually consecrates sight with feeling, and this is heightened by a spectral presence in the atmosphere. This enriched perception, which plumps out even the late fruits of the landscape, is far less a Freudian overvaluation than an expression of poetic love, by which the poet both humanizes the spectre and suggests his own self-acceptance. When, in reading *A Midsummer Night's Dream,* Keats came upon Titania's mention of a "middle summer's spring" (II, i, 82), his response was immediate and enthusiastic: "There is something exquisitely rich and luxurious in Titania's saying 'since the middle summer's spring' as if Bowers were not exuberant and covert enough for fairy sports untill their second sprouting—which is surely the most bounteous overwhelming of all Nature's goodnesses. She steps forth benignly in the spring and her conduct is so gracious that by degrees all things are becoming happy under her wings and nestle against her bosom: she feels this love and gratitude too much to remain selfsame, and unable to contain herself buds forth the overflowings of her heart. . . ." [16] To see the threat in the personification yet still to allow such spontaneous "overflowings" of powerful feeling is the way by which the capable imagination makes relationship possible. Presence is perhaps only an idea, but it is necessary to these imaginings. It seems to demand repression, but the poet responds as if it approves and forgives the mediating ego. If Yeats is right that all great literature is the forgiveness of sin, we might look for the source of forgiveness to the poet's affirmation of an emotional existence, in the face of a repressive ideal he himself necessarily summons.

THE TRYSTING-PLACE: "THE FALL OF HYPERION. A DREAM"

In this dialogue there are no final victories, nor can there be. Yeats confessed that he soliloquized all day long.[17] Keats, though by temperament a less subjective man, nevertheless could not help beginning dialogue anew with each fresh poetic start. The richness of the fifth stanza of the *Ode to a Nightingale* and of the whole of *To Autumn* are myths of presence, or fictions of relationship. As such, the intensity can be dissipated by "pathetic" thoughts (which terminate encounters) or egotistical self-possession (here follows declamatory prose). Keats, as the extraordinary poet he was, seeks the meeting place of self and other, the scene in which the power of presence may be made accessible to the poet's feelingful perception. The poet here must concede priority to otherness, but indirectly he proves that without his own presence the sublime other would have no priority. In other words, he needs the heightening that the sublime provides, but he completes or defines that sublimity as he engages it. This, broadly, is the relationship portrayed in *The Fall of Hyperion,* one of the most magnificent poems Keats wrote (even if in some need of revision, and if fragmentary), and one of the most moving in the language.

The poem was written for the most part between July and September, 1819, and represents Keats's attempt to revise the earlier *Hyperion* along the lines suggested by his current views on the concerns that continued to fascinate him: the discrepancy between poetic truth and dreaming, the role the poet plays in the amelioration of human suffering, and the relation of poetic inspiration to the presence of an otherness that includes the idea of the parent—though this is general and itself includes poetic precursors. These central issues, together with a more Dantean mood, led Keats to substitute himself as poetic speaker for the earlier Apollo, thereby making possible the encounter form, which had come to be his most dramatically powerful poetic mode.

Most of the fictions and the evasions are gone as the poem opens, except for those that will be given up by both the poet and Monetá in their dialogue, and except for those fictions that are not so much fictions as articles of faith. What is being examined and tested in the poem is meaning, including the meaning the poet confers upon the past as a way of establishing relationship to it and so drawing it into his present. How real are large-limbed visions, how meaningful are the huge, cloudy symbols of romance? Can the poet survive as poet, or perhaps as man, without these? The questions the poem raises are manifold. But with the fictions disappearing before our eyes, with the poet making a supreme effort to retain only what may suffice, there are more implied answers or at least resting points for speculation in *The Fall* than in any other poem Keats wrote.

The central themes are introduced in an induction (ll. 1–18) that is remarkably compressed yet contains elements we have traced throughout Keats's poetry. Both "Fanatics" and savages construct images of paradise based on their "dreams," the poet begins, but these have been lost because they never were recorded "upon vellum or wild Indian leaf."

> For Poesy alone can tell her dreams,
> With the fine spell of words alone can save
> Imagination from the sable charm
> And dumb enchantment. Who alive can say,
> "Thou art no poet; may'st not tell thy dreams"?
> Since every man whose soul is not a clod
> Hath visions, and would speak, if he had loved
> And been well nurtured in his mother tongue.

Enchantment, which Keats as poet had feared almost from the beginnings of his career, emerges as a corollary to death, "the sable charm." The life of the "Imagination" is saved by Poesy, though we note the curious charm, countercharm relationship she has with death, since she herself uses the "fine spell of words"—a white magic against a black. A Shakespearean idea, we might be tempted to say: that poetry can preserve the imagination for future generations. And Keats, of course, loved the sonnets, in which one meets the idea frequently. But this is a poem that questions "Imagination" in its sense of the image-making faculty. As a deep and severe examination of poetic meaning, *The Fall* brings into question the nature and purpose of poetic images, and thus of the way poets "read" reality. Finally, the question is one of language, but of a poet's language and his related beliefs. The past impinges so greatly on these that though it is indeed true that no one "alive" can deprive a man of his poethood, it is not so clear that the *dead* cannot. Every man has "visions," it may be, but those in the poem are sublime in scope and content—they image a past. In any case, every man would speak of his visions "if he had loved." This has from the outset been the prerequisite to poetic voice in Keats, though the poet now explicitly adds being nurtured in the "mother tongue" as an additional condition. "Mother tongue" is in itself parental, but it also, as the poem develops, specifically suggests the tongue of Moneta, whose voice is that of the sublime, but who tempers her words for the poet: "As near as an immortal's spherèd words / Could to a mother's soften" (I, 249–50). The two referents of "mother tongue" straddle the dialectic of sublimity and humanization that runs through the poem.

It is in the sublime that the poet has been nurtured, but his experience in *The Fall* is intended to separate him from such great expectations. The form of the poem is that of a dream within a dream, in which the poet unwillingly progresses from an Eden-like bower to the sanctuary of the Titans, where he encounters Moneta and the strictures of purgation. The narrative proper begins with the characteristic "Methought," a signal that we have entered the realm of dream: "Methought I stood where trees of every clime" made "a screen" (I, 19, 21). Keats's language is so highly metaphoric in the poem that, with the advantage of a knowledge of what is to come, we see the irony in the poet's initial sense of self. "Methought I stood" reverberates with upcoming falls, that of the Titans and that of the poet's own loss of Eden. It is useful at this early point to introduce the notion that the narrative of the poem is also an allegory for the poet's own history, which begins with the pleasant illusion that one stands protectively screened by the trees of tradition. The scene also includes the mossy retreat of all romance, the bower that seems so like Eden:

> on a mound
> Of moss, was spread a feast of summer fruits,
> Which, nearer seen, seemed refuse of a meal
> By angel tasted, or our Mother Eve.
>
> [I, 28–31]

The angel or our grandparent has parted, however, as if the poet were born into belatedness. These are the foods "whose pure kinds I could not know" (I, 34), though the scene awakens in the poet a yearning that closely parallels a desire for beauty. The fact that he has come upon the scene too late to be a part of it must be a factor in the growing appetite he feels, but be that as it may, eating the food brings on thirst, and there is at hand a deceptive drink: nearby

> Stood a cool vessel of transparent juice,
> Sipped by the wandered bee, the which I took,
> And, pledging all the mortals of the world,
> And all the dead whose names are in our lips,
> Drank. That full draught is parent of my theme.
> No Asian poppy, nor elixir fine
> . . . .
> Could so have rapt unwilling life away.
> Among the fragrant husks and berries crushed,
> Upon the grass I struggled hard against
> The domineering potion; but in vain.
>
> [I, 42–47, 51–54]

The potion, like Cynthia in *Endymion,* threatens to extinguish natural, "unwilling life," and is "domineering" in the same way that the "shady visions" in the earlier *Hyperion* came to domineer. Both Cynthia and the visions suggest the sublime, and it is this that the poet claims is the "parent" of his theme. How metaphoric is his use of the word? As we glance back over Keats's career—as he himself is doing in this farewell to Eden and romance—we may conclude that the sublime has often been the metaphoric parent of his themes. But the potion as an agent of sublimity proleptically reminds us of Moneta and also of Saturn, the sublime figures who are about to appear in the poem and who play the role of parents to a poetic son.

When the poet recovers from the draught, he finds he has lost the "mossy mound" and the arbor: they "were no more" (I, 60). Pledging the mortals of the world and reaching for the power of the elixir transforms his scene to an ancient "sanctuary," no longer Psyche's but Saturn's.

> I raised
> My eyes to fathom the space every way—
> The embossed roof, the silent massy range
> Of columns north and south, ending in mist
> Of nothing, then to eastward, where black gates
> Were shut against the sunrise evermore.
> Then to the west I looked, and saw far off
> An image, huge of feature as a cloud.
>
> [I, 81–88]

This is a holy place, yet it manifests dread: the "mist / Of nothing" reminds us of the reiterated nothings that Endymion feared his dream would become, a truth of which Peona was convinced. There is no reflex of egotism here, merely acceptance of a place that has shut out fresh beginnings with the sunrise and that, like the conclusion of Wordsworth's *Intimations* ode, is moving inexorably westward, with the clouds that gather around the setting sun. At this point, the poet's upraised eyes are arrested by "An image" of sublime dimension but which the poet has trouble "reading." The mistiness and the clouded features create an amorphousness that makes it difficult for the poet to "fathom" the space. Thus begins his attempt to read or interpret the sublime, which he continues through the balance of the poem as we have it. We note that even in the Edenic bower what seemed from a distance to be "a feast of summer fruits" when "nearer seen" appeared to be the "refuse" of

the meal of an angel, or of Eve. The nature of vision, as the
poet seeks a god's sight, involves the elemental questions of
desire and meaning that the poem poses.

  Keats in the *Ode to Psyche* lamented the loss of those early
days when one could believe, "Holy the air, the water and
the fire." Now he has come at last to the scene of the "Holy
Power" (I, 136) that is Moneta, the trysting-place where late
poets meet their predecessors, familial and poetic. Moneta's
first words to the poet are as harshly threatening as any stric-
ture of the ego ideal—"If thou canst not ascend / These
steps, die on that marble where thou art" (I, 107–08)—but
the poet survives and enters a dialogue in which he gives to
the most doubting questions of poetry and the poet the most
chastened replies. In response to Moneta's warning that only
those who understand the misery of the world can "usurp"—
a word which makes us pause, since there has recently been
a devastating usurpation in heaven—her high place, the poet
questions his solitary presence, and his relation to love:

> "Are there not thousands in the world," said I,
> Encouraged by the sooth voice of the shade,
> "Who love their fellows even to the death;
> Who feel the giant agony of the world;
> And more, like slaves to poor humanity,
> Labour for mortal good? I sure should see
> Other men here: but I am here alone."
>
> [I, 154–60]

  The poet questions a love like Saturn's in the earlier version of the poem: loving until death, feeling the agony of existence—these are the self-surrenders that result in a slavish
devotion to the great cause. He senses that Moneta demands
this submission, which is not wholly uncharacteristic of him,
since we know that he pledged all poor mortals in drinking
the elixir. But Moneta converts the possible victory of "I am
here alone" to a further need for expiation. The poet is here
alone, she replies, because the other lovers of humanity are
not "visionaries," they are not "dreamers weak" (I, 161, 162).
But she judges the poet who stands before her to be "a

dreaming thing" and advises him to "Think of the earth" (I, 168, 169). Her words are so compelling, and his need for her speech so genuine and moving, that we may forget the circumstances and the consequent irony. Indeed he is a dreaming thing, and the poem itself, as its subtitle states, is a dream. She does not exist apart from that dream, which is not to say that she is merely a fiction so much as to say that she needs his power of dreaming to give definition to the high tragedy she represents. It is, then, a further irony that she wants him to think only of the earth. Her advice is intended to dispel his belief in epiphany, to have him give up any dream of heaven. She, the fallen Titan, insists that he send away once for all the parting genius and all gods. In her view, the earth is quickly replacing lost heaven, and the altar is the sacrificial place that proclaims only pathos. But he cannot give up some amount of dreaming, some need for epiphany and the presence of otherness, which indeed has led him to this sanctuary. In an extraordinary inversion of the sublime, and an equally astonishing reversal of the poetic role usual in Keats, Moneta affirms pathos as the only truth of existence, and the poet modestly implies the necessity of the sublime, the epiphanic otherness that *is* the holiness he seeks, and without which there is no poetic love. The notion of a simple slavery to weak humanity would require a submission the poet would rather not make, though he is ready to uplift that very humanity with his love: hence his pledge in Eden is not so much a gesture of self-sacrifice as a promise.

We now can see somewhat more clearly the complexities inherent in the relation of the poet to the sublime other. Endymion had taken in "draughts of life" from his encounter with Cynthia, which sublimed him from the vale of life and all its cares. Keats's own increasingly emotional trend led him to resist this sublimation (not a psychoanalytic sublimation, of course), and to view it as a threat that is relieved by the sorrow and pathos of the Indian Maiden, whom the poet identifies with Cynthia, as a means of bringing the sublime down to earth, as it were. *The Fall of Hyperion* seems to suggest another side of this relationship, in which the poet needs the parental holiness of the sublime and the large-limbed visions it makes possible. His belief, his love, require that spectral presence, that heightening of imagination. The sublime, for its part, now appears to have assimilated a culture of the death instinct, as Freud might term this, though I myself would rather leave the instinctual element out of the identification. Moneta is a parental figure who has not achieved heaven, merely a kind of dark purgatory, and who furthermore tries to dissuade the poet who is still in search of his poetic identity from expectations that he will excell her meager end. It is this sorrowful truth that the poet must redeem—the poet quite genuinely now, as Keats tells Moneta, as "humanist, physician to all men" (I, 190). Not just a humanization, but a redemption of the sublime becomes necessary as otherness and pathos become increasingly indistinguishable.

I therefore think we should not overestimate Moneta's grasp of truth when she confidently tells the poet the distinction between poetry and dreaming:

> "Art thou not of the dreamer tribe?
> The poet and the dreamer are distinct
> Diverse, sheer opposite, antipodes."
>
> [I, 198–200]

It is not true that the two are "antipodes": certainly the poet who is only a dreamer can never claim our admiration, but the view that dreaming is not a part of poetry must be based on error. When the dream of otherness is over, poetry of this order is over, and the poet's task must be to resist pure pathos as well as the purely antithetical sublime. Moneta and Saturn embody that pathos and therefore that danger:

> "this old image here,
> Whose carvèd features wrinkled as he fell,
> Is Saturn's: I, Moneta, left supreme,
> Sole priestess of his desolation."
> I had no words to answer, for my tongue,

> Useless, could find about its roofed home
> No syllable of a fit majesty
> To make rejoinder to Moneta's mourn.
>
> [I, 224–31]

What is it that stills the poet's tongue which, we infer, is not yet nurtured? Moneta introduces herself as the priestess of Saturn's "desolation." That pathetic condition finally has found a spokesman: in the *Grecian Urn* ode what moved the poet to surrender the vision was the absence of anyone to tell why that little town had been made desolate. More importantly, desolation, as Moneta begins to describe it, consists of the dissolution of the "old image" that is Saturn, as what once had been "carvèd," as if permanently, falls into merely earthly old age. And yet the poet has come to the sanctuary to find an image sufficiently huge of feature to compensate for the loss of his early "Eden." The connection between sublimity and language lies in the image of Saturn, which the poet, as part of his poetic education and his growth in consciousness, must recognize is fading.

The loss of the sublime image becomes increasingly important in the poem, and we shall return to this central theme. Moneta offers the poet in its place the power to see "scenes" (I, 244) which represent a pure consciousness, that is, a consciousness of pathos, of the self increasingly approaching death. But before she does so she must mitigate the terror the poet has of her, by unveiling her face. This is a climactic revelation in Keats's poetry, for penetrating the mystery has been a central concern at least since the appearance of the charioteer in *Sleep and Poetry*, whose writing Keats could not see.

> Then saw I a wan face,
> Not pined by human sorrows, but bright-blanched
> By an immortal sickness which kills not.
> It works a constant change, which happy death
> Can put no end to; deathwards progressing
> To no death was that visage; it had passed
> The lily and the snow; and beyond these

I must not think now, though I saw that face—
But for her eyes I should have fled away.
They held me back, with a benignant light,
Soft-mitigated by divinest lids
Half-closed, and visionless entire they seemed
Of all external things—they saw me not,
But in blank splendour beamed like the mild moon,
Who comforts those she sees not, who knows not
What eyes are upward cast.

[I, 256–71]

Moneta's wan countenance reflects the continuity into which she has fallen, and this is turned to contradiction by her godly deathlessness: she is in "constant change" and progresses inexorably to a death she cannot die. She nevertheless is beyond life—the lily and the snow can no longer be invoked as comparisons for her paleness. Moneta is the presence who is dying except to the mind, she is the dream that cannot be surrendered, and her aspect threatens to end the telling of the poem in the "now" in which it is written, but the poet pulls back from the "beyond" she has reached. His seeing ("though I saw that face") is partial and self-protective: it is not yet the depthful but paralyzing vision of Moneta.

This gentle turn from Moneta's deathly reality continues as the poet responds to her eyes. Like the poet himself in the *Ode to Psyche*, Moneta is by her own eyes inspired; hers is the blindness that for a long time he has feared he would have to accept. She exists apart from him, as from all external things, and she is suggestive of those who have gone before him: she is not only motheral, but her "benignant" light recalls Wordsworth's hope, expressed in the Prospectus to *The Excursion*, that his "Song / With starlike virtue in its place may shine / Shedding benignant influence" (ll. 88–90); and her blind, "blank splendour" takes us back once more to Milton's complaint for his blindness, which leaves him with only "a universal blank" (*Paradise Lost*, III, 48). The poet softens this composite darkness by finding again a similitude with the moon: her eyes "beamed like the mild moon, / Who com-

forts those she sees not." This is one of Keats's earliest figures of comfort, as in "Fill for me a brimming bowl," written
in 1814: "The melting softness of that face, / The beaminess
of those bright eyes" (ll. 14–15). The brightness is shadowy
now, and the poet does not attempt to internalize or sublimate. Moneta dwells apart, she "knows not" what eyes are
cast upward to her. The poet knows this, knows that though
she is his muse and always has been she can teach him only a
deathly continuity, yet he finds in her a benignant light, a
soft mitigation. This is an effort to achieve a genuinely humanized sublime, purchased with the cost of an acknowledged distance yet with the tentative reward of some comfort yet.

That comfort lasts but a moment, for the poet needs to
know the nature of Moneta's inward vision, and to realize
her promise of making her power accessible to him. He receives both of these, though as he does so the "image" that in
the poem has been identified with the sublime finally gives
way to a godlike vision:

> I looked beneath the gloomy boughs,
> And saw, what first I thought an image huge,
> Like to the image pedestalled so high
> In Saturn's temple. Then Moneta's voice
> Came brief upon my ear: "So Saturn sat
> When he had lost his realms." Whereon there grew
> A power within me of enormous ken
> To see as a god sees, and take the depth
> Of things as nimbly as the outward eye
> Can size and shape pervade. The lofty theme
> At those few words hung vast before my mind,
> With half-unravelled web. I set myself
> Upon an eagle's watch, that I might see,
> And seeing ne'er forget. No stir of life
> Was in this shrouded vale.
>
> [I, 297–311]

The poet had come in search of a sublimity that would sustain the imagination. Thus his initial error: he thinks of Saturn as an "image huge." But the sublime scale is a fiction or

evasion, for Moneta's voice, like other voices we have encountered in the poetry, interrupts his surmise with the
truth that this is the Saturn who has "lost his realms," not the
god whose presence is also a promise. And so the power to
see as a god sees, which replaces the sublime "image" ("size
and shape") with the ability to "take the depth / Of things."
This is Wordsworthian, for *Tintern Abbey* describes vision as
the power to "see into the life of things" (1. 49). And it provides the poet with his proper "depth," sought throughout
Endymion.

The poet sees at once his "lofty theme," but this treats a
breaking of images, and these have always been for him
what the eye that was threatened with extinction saw. When
Endymion cried out for Cynthia not to destroy his "sovereign vision," we sense that he meant also his vision as a sovereign. Moneta's "few words" imply that the truth of vision is
that realms are lost, and it is this understanding, emblemed
in the vale, that the poet tries to see and "ne'er forget."
Remembrance, once of outer things, now is of things passing, and the power to see brings a sight of the loss of power:
there is no "stir of life" in Saturn's shrouded vale.

Keats's devotion now is to a deadly belief that the image
must necessarily be replaced by the reality of loss—that the
sublime must yield to the pathetic. Moneta's vision does not
mingle contraries nor allow departures from the overwhelm-
ingness of loss. This is the nadir of the imagination, but the
poet must survive it though it offers no possibility of life-giving change:

> Without stay or prop
> But my own weak mortality, I bore
> The load of this eternal quietude,
> The unchanging gloom, and the three fixèd shapes
> Ponderous upon my senses a whole moon.
> For by my burning brain I measured sure
> Her silver seasons shedded on the night,
> And every day by day methought I grew
> More gaunt and ghostly. Oftentimes I prayed

> Intense, that death would take me from the vale
> And all its burthens. Gasping with despair
> Of change, hour after hour I cursed myself.
>
> [I, 388–99]

This is a mercilessly antithetical reality, which threatens to overwhelm the senses not with bliss but the weight of continuous time that precludes digression. The poet is frozen into the posture of Imogen or Calliope, for what is happening as he grows more daemonically ghostly, as he curses his lack of power, is that he is losing the poetic faculty and the redeeming power of poetic love: when Saturn calls for "Beautiful things made new" Keats hears only the voice of mortality:

> Methought I heard some old man of the earth
> Bewailing earthly loss; nor could my eyes
> And ears act with that pleasant unison of sense
> Which marries sweet sound with the grace of form,
> And dolorous accent from a tragic harp
> With large-limbed visions.
>
> [I, 440–45]

Pathos alone cannot sustain the poetic imagination. Nor, ironically, can mortality. The image-making power breaks down as Saturn speaks as merely a man, and the poet loses the ability to reconcile the sublimer visual image with its apparently contradictory meaning. The poet as poet needs these large-limbed visions, these cloudy symbols of romance, for he needs for his imaginings the illusory dignity of the family romance—Freud's name for the child's fiction that his true parents are grander than his real ones seem. This is a necessary grandeur, but the reality seems to the poet to suggest only death: Saturn, like the earlier nightingale, is "buried" and cannot exercise "influence benign" upon those who follow (I, 413, 414).

It is this "load" that the poet must bear, if only with his own mortality. Saturn is in the midst of becoming only another of the dead whose names are in our lips; the poet must reconcile himself with eternal quietude. This I think he begins to do in the second canto, which is, however, incomplete. Guesses as to where the poem might have gone are quite useless, and in fact distract us from the real possibility that the poem is finished—not in a narrative but in a thematic sense. From the deep vale of mortality the poet rises to Hyperion in the heavens, caught in the moment before his fall. His "sovereignty" (II, 14) is in jeopardy, but its existence is sufficient for the poet to cast off the darkness: "Now in clear light I stood, / Relieved from the dusk vale" (II, 49–50). He no longer stands where trees of every clime shelter Eden's mossy mound, but he stands again, and his senses synesthetically take in a renewed life, as the mere earth of Saturn gives way to the oxymoron of Hyperion:

> My quick eyes ran on
> From stately nave to nave, from vault to vault,
> Through bowers of fragrant and enwreathèd light
> And diamond-pavèd lustrous long arcades.
> Anon rushed by the bright Hyperion;
> His flaming robes streamed out beyond his heels,
> And gave a roar, as if of earthly fire.
>
> [II, 53–59]

Throughout his encounter with Moneta, the poet has had to soften her even as she has had to chasten his desire. This portrait of Hyperion, which allows the god briefly to retain his heaven while glancing at the coming darkness of earth, is the poet's achieved vision and contains less than the emotions desire but more than the intellect believes. It would be reductive to identify Moneta only with the ego ideal, or to see the poet's ongoing dialogue with her as the difficult avenue to Unity of Being. Yet these identities inform both Moneta and the conclusion of the poem, in which the humanizing imagination once more becomes able to reconcile the severity of the antithetical with the emotional, the sublime with pathos, one's own death and one's self-forgiveness, in a momentary perfection that joins contraries—Hyperion's "earthly fire." Neither wholly a god nor yet a man of earth, Hyperion stands, even as the poet does, at the meeting place of self and other, and achieves an innocence that, though not as cleansing as Yeats's in the epigraph, yet enables him to continue. We know that his fire is waning, that his future course is downward to the darkness of the vale, but Keats allows him a brief horizontal movement that concludes with nobleness both the poem and a career: "On he flared. . . ."

5

Coda: Yeats's Dialogues with the
Voice of Enchantment

> *The Lay of the Last Minstrel* gave me a wish to turn magician that competed for years with the dream of being killed upon the seashore.
>
> Yeats, *Reveries over Childhood and Youth*

The path to the "trysting-place," where poetic voice becomes intensely lyrical, is particularly full of traps in Yeats. It is Yeats, of course, who has provided us with the term, and it is apparent that from quite early both a rendezvous and its consequent Unity of Being are poetic ideals. Nevertheless, for the reader the problems of reading Yeats are many. One cause of difficulty is the evolution Yeats's theory and practice undergo during his long career. The central elements that comprise Keats's poetic—the difficulty in identifying the nature of otherness, the opposition between identification as a mode of internalization and the repression required by an antithetical ideal—are to be found in Yeats as well; and development follows a course from idealization to a more emotional posture; but the extremes of opposition and development are greater in Yeats. Following the path in brief therefore may seem a hopeless enterprise, but even a quick view may do to map directions and sketch the ground traversed.

Yeats's early idealism centers on the relation of transcendent and earthly realms, and the possible communication between these. In 1898 he takes as almost an article of faith the inscription of the Emerald Tablet of Hermes: "The things below are as the things above." [1] This relation informs a statement that might be a credo of the early years:

> Can there be anything so important as to cry out that what we call romance, poetry, intellectual beauty, is the only signal that the supreme Enchanter, or someone in His councils, is speaking of what has been, and shall be again, in the consummation of time? [2]

Like Milton's Attendant Spirit or like Keats in a number of poems, Yeats surmises a voice that speaks above of what poetry speaks below. These shall meet, not precisely at the midnight hour, but in the consummation of time, which suggests not only finality but marriage. Yeats was fond of thinking that every man has a central and recurrent myth or image, and this early statement of a poetic ideal comes as close to capturing Yeats's "myth" as almost anything he writes.

Symbols mediate between these realms. Or rather, since they are a part of our world, they are ways up, they are boundary figures. But for Yeats there are two kinds of symbol and two corresponding relations to the world. The reader who encounters symbols that are "merely emotional," he writes in 1900, "gazes from amid the accidents and destinies of the world; but if the symbols are intellectual too, he becomes himself a part of pure intellect, and he is himself mingled with the procession." [3] The *intellectual* symbol offers the possibility of a "becoming" that implies a movement from self to the region that Yeats sees as beyond both the self and the world. It is this desire for otherness that characterizes Yeats's early idealism: he observes that if, for example, he looks at the moon and remembers "any of her ancient names and meanings, I move among divine people, and things that have shaken off our mortality. . . ." Yeats sees in Shakespeare a poet who has chosen an *emotional* symbology in an effort to draw the reader to the natural world, whereas Dante is the rare poet who has given up the world and formulated intellectual symbols. Thus, if one is moved by Shakespeare, "who is content with emotional symbols that he may come the nearer to our sympathy, one is mixed with the whole spectacle of the world; while if one is moved by Dante, or by the myth of Demeter, one is mixed into the shadow of God or of a goddess." [4]

The conflict between the spectacle of the world and the distant region of divinity leads Yeats to conclude that there are two forms of poetic vision, one based upon the world and natural existence, and one that renounces all that is natural. William Morris serves Yeats as an example of a "happy" poet, one who has chosen to honor body and what Yeats calls the Green Tree of natural plenitude. Yeats admires Morris, yet shows an inability to sympathize fully with a world that is only natural. Morris, as we have seen, seems to Yeats always to tell the same story, of "how some man or woman lost and found again the happiness that is always half of the body," and his poetry "often wearies us as the unbroken green of July wearies us, for there is something in us, some bitterness because of the Fall, it may be, that takes a little from the sweetness of Eve's apple after the first mouthful." [5] In Shakespeare, in this instance, Yeats finds a countervision that rescues idealism or the absolute, though it does so at the expense of the world: Shakespeare "meditated as Solomon, not as Bentham meditated, upon blind ambitions, untoward accidents, and capricious passions, and the world was almost as empty in his eyes as it must be in the eyes of God." [6]

In his own career, Yeats progresses from an antinatural, intellectual poetic to a sense that the world must find its place in poetic imaginings—those that in 1900 he refers to as "emotional." The progression reflects a division that is present in Yeats from the outset, and which even the later radical conceptions of mask and daemon could not heal. When in his youth he attended meetings of the Rhymers' Club, as he informs us, "I remember praying that I might get my imagination fixed upon life itself," but that focus always slipped away, for "in those days I was a convinced ascetic." [7] This strain of asceticism, which precludes the possibility of the imagination choosing "life itself," is the parent of Yeats's intellectual idealism; both represent reflex responses to a sudden awareness that Yeats identifies as the moment of nativity of the subjective poet: "a hero loves the world till it breaks him, and the poet till it has broken faith." [8]

Poetic subjectivity begins with this pervasive sense. As we have seen with Keats, the expression of subjectivity as a poetic can take either of two forms following object-loss: the identification that is a variety of sublimation, or the repression that accompanies the choice of an antithetical ideal. It is clear that in these early years, as he remembers them, Yeats's feeling that a covenant has been broken leads him to choose a difficult idealism, despite his prayers for a relationship between imagination and emotional life. Idealism in effect becomes a substitute for the world that breaks faith, and asceticism a measure of devotion. The renunciatory aspect of this situation finds a partial explanation in Freud's notion of *idealization,* that version of love in which "the object"—here the subject of the idealism—"is being treated in the same way as our own ego, so that . . . a considerable amount of narcissistic libido overflows onto the object. It is even obvious . . . that the object serves as a substitute for some unattained ego ideal of our own." As love and devotion increase, Freud finds the ego making a "self-sacrifice" to the object, which now owns much of its love.[9] Though Freud's vocabulary differs from Yeats's, "self-sacrifice" as renunciation lies near the heart of the poet's early vision, as Yeats's remembrance of his asceticism implies.

Yeats's idealism reflects a hope for sublimity, though as with Keats and the charioteer in *Sleep and Poetry,* Yeats at this early time sees the sublime as other, a possible sublimity mixing with a possible poetic identity. That possible identity is most often Shelley's, the singer of *"intellectual* beauty," and the subject of the very important essay *The Philosophy of Shelley's Poetry* (1900). On one level, however, the essay is concerned with Yeats's hope that he is the inheritor of Shelley's idealism, and that consequently he will be mingled in the procession of voices that Shelley once heard. Yeats characterizes Shelley as one of the "children of desire," where de-

sire is infinite, and in a startling reverie, sees Keats in love
with the changeable moon, Blake with the sun that is all
energy, but Shelley wandering "in some chapel of the Star of
infinite desire," where

> voices would have told him how there is for every man
> some one scene . . . that is the image of his secret life,
> for wisdom first speaks in images, and that this one
> image, if he would but brood over it his life long, would
> lead his soul, disentangled from the ebb and flow of the
> world, into that far household where the undying gods
> await all whose souls have become simple as flame,
> whose bodies have become quiet as an agate lamp.[10]

Shelley, the antithetical poet, listens to those voices of supreme enchantment that promise—if his desire is great
enough—the coming of wisdom in the consummation of
time. Their promise realizes the desire of the antithetical or
antinatural poet to be sublimed, to be made one with otherness.

Yeats's marvelous prose is distinctive, yet the idea itself is
common to much contemplative poetry since Milton.
Wordsworth characteristically mutes a contemplative moment in which the body sleeps as the soul becomes flame:

> that serene and blessed mood,
> In which the affections gently lead us on,—
> Until, the breath of this corporeal frame
> And even the motion of our human blood
> Almost suspended, we are laid asleep
> In body, *and become a living soul.*
> [*Tintern Abbey*, 41–46; my emphasis]

Wordsworth draws back from an extreme antinaturalism—
the body, in his description, is only "laid asleep"—but Yeats's
idea of the soul passing to the "far household" of divinity, as
the reader of intellectual symbols is mixed into the shadow
of the gods, is an antithetical idea and relies upon a transcendence of all that is natural. The "image" that wisdom
discloses to Shelley is also sought by Yeats's antithetical

questers—"I seek an image not a book," Ille proclaims in *Ego Dominus Tuus*—because there is in a contemplated image a suggestion of an intellectual symbol. Yeats thought that during inspiration Shelley made of this relationship an identity:

> he must have expected to receive thoughts and images from beyond his own mind, just in so far as that mind transcended its preoccupation with particular time and place, for he believed inspiration a kind of death; and he could hardly have helped perceiving that an image that has transcended particular time and place becomes a symbol, passes beyond death, as it were, *and becomes a living soul.*[11]

The passage from image to symbol and thus to a Wordsworthian "living soul" (there seems little doubt that Wordsworth is at least the verbal source here), is thus central to Yeats's early thought. In this phase of the poetic development we are trying to trace, the passage or "becoming" lies behind his admiration for Shelley's Intellectual Beauty and antithetical quest:

> had *Prince Athanase* been finished it would have described the finding of Pandemos, the Star's lower genius, and the growing weary of her, and the coming of its true genius Urania at the coming of death, as the day finds the Star at evening.[12]

Here, however, is the rub for the poet who has chosen a severe ideal: the "consummation" that unites below and above is identified in this surmise as death. Pandemos and Urania are as world and divinity or emotion and intellect, and though the poet's idealizing tendency leads him to choose the latter, the choice can suddenly become a threat to existence. Thoughts of self may intrude, as they seem to have upon Yeats, as he writes in 1906 in *Discoveries*.

What Yeats "discovers" in this later essay is his separation from the sublimity of otherness, and so himself. In writing of his early desire for "impersonal beauty," Yeats recalls achieving what he wants us to see as a self-recognition:

> Then one day I understood quite suddenly, as the way is, that I was seeking something unchanging and unmixed and always outside myself, a Stone or an Elixir that was always out of reach, and that *I myself* was the fleeting thing that held out its hand.[13]

What is "unmixed" and beyond the self is Shelley's intellectual beauty, which Yeats now pejoratively terms "impersonal." It is not that the changing world passes before the fixed contemplative mind, but that the world is permanent and the mind fleeting, and with this discovery Yeats begins to turn from Shelley's intellectualism to the sensuous and the emotional, from a severe idealism to the emotional return of identification. "And so it was I entered the broken world," is Hart Crane's version of self-recognition, by which he means "And so it was I became broken," and Yeats's discovery of self similarly is tinged with a recognition of mortality. Involved here, as in Keats's mode of internalization, is the poet's capacity for self-acceptance. The antithetical idealism that Yeats now thinks of as a quest for an absolute and impossible beauty overcomes the emotional self and evades this necessary acceptance, which grows increasingly important in Yeats. Though Yeats recalls that he gave up the earlier quest "one day" and began a new relationship to outer things, it would be a mistake to regard these quests as covering separate periods of his life. Keats wrote the *Ode to Psyche* and the *Ode to a Nightingale* in the same month; Yeats similarly turns and returns to the antithetical ideal throughout his career. The object of Unity of Being now becomes a union of the two spheres.

In *Discoveries* Yeats explicitly rejects anything distant, anything "out of reach," as the proper subject of poetry, and consequently rejects the contemplative mode.

> All art is sensuous, but when a man puts only his contemplative nature and his more *vague* desires into his art, the sensuous images through which it speaks become broken, fleeting, uncertain, or are chosen for their *distance* from general experience, and all grows unsubstantial and *fantastic*.[14]

Yeats wrote *The Philosophy of Shelley's Poetry* in part to rescue Shelley from the charge of being a *"vague* thinker, who mixed occasional great poetry with a *fantastic* rhetoric," [15] but *Discoveries* moves inexorably toward a repudiation of Shelley on just these grounds. From this seemingly general point of view—that the basis of art should not be the artist's "contemplative nature and his more vague desires"—Yeats arrives at a consideration of Shelley in particular. In Shelley's poetic world, Yeats now claims, "I lacked something to compensate my imagination for geographical and historical reality . . . and found myself wishing for and trying to imagine . . . a crowd of believers who could put into all those strange sights the strength of their belief. . . ." The soul needs symbolic art, but all symbolic art "should arise out of a real belief," and it is here that Shelley fails:

> I am certain that there are many who are not moved as they would be by that solitary light burning in the tower of Prince Athanase, because it has not entered into men's prayers nor lighted any through the sacred dark of religious contemplation. [16]

A fundamental problem for Yeats as a modern poet is that "contemplation" has separated itself from the "emotions common to all." In contrast, the earliest artists, Homer and Hesiod, might combine both passion and religious contemplation; their common and familiar "places" might "have changed before the poem's end to symbols and vanished. . . ." But those days were "unbroken"—then a poet "could have all the subtlety of Shelley, and yet use no image unknown among the common people. . . ." Even Shakespeare's "journeys to Rome or to Verona" now seem to Yeats to be an "out-flowing of an unrest, a dissatisfaction with natural interests," and he concludes with a new credo:

> I am orthodox and pray for a resurrection of the body, and am certain that a man should find his Holy Land where he first crept upon the floor, and that familiar woods and rivers should fade into symbol with so gradual a change that he may never discover, no not even in

ecstasy itself, that he is beyond space, and that time
alone keeps him from Primum Mobile, Supernal Eden,
Yellow Rose over all.[17]

We recognize, in Yeats's "fading into symbol," a continuity
with the early idea of passing into the region of the intellectual symbol, but Yeats wants us to see a difference, for here
the "resurrection" is of familiar things, which are not left
behind but subtly transformed. Has Yeats retrieved the symbol from the intellect and diminished its distance from ordinary experience? One wonders how far from Shelley's
sacred dark Yeats has come in fact, for despite his conviction
that Shelley had entered an abyss of idealism, one recalls
that Yeats had proclaimed in the essay of 1900 that Shelley's
"beauty," into which all things should pass, comprises a
"kind of resurrection of the body." [18]

If we nevertheless avoid for the moment this ambiguity of
poetic influence, we may ask what is signified by Yeats's desire to abandon contemplation for "emotion" or passion.
When he looks back upon those years that seem to corre-
spond to a first phase of development, he regrets that he
"was interested in nothing but states of mind, lyrical moments, intellectual essences." In contrast, he cites the "sweetness" and the "rhythmic movement" that "there is in those
who have become the joy that is themselves." The transition
from "intellectual essences" and "impersonal beauty" to the
"joy" that is one's emotional self seems to comprise Yeats's
idea of coming to a self-understanding.

With this version of what Keats might call a journey homeward to self, Yeats abandons a monistic, substitutive idealism
in favor of a dualistic poetic that attempts to include both
emotion and intellect, self-presence and idealism. We arrive,
then, at Yeats's theoretical formulations of daemon and
mask, together one of the most dangerous traps for the
reader. The poet assumes the mask to engage or summon
the daemon, and the daemon represents the antithetical
ideal, the otherness the poet invokes in quest of wholeness.
This much is reasonably clear, but the mask's aesthetic and

psychological significances are difficult to discern. One of Yeats's more illuminating comments on both the mask and the process of psychological identification—though of course he does not so name it—is found in one of those suggestive recollections that fill the *Autobiography.* "As life goes on," he writes, "we discover that certain thoughts sustain us in defeat, or give us victory. . . ."

> Among subjective men . . . the victory is an *intellectual* daily re-creation of all that exterior fate snatches away, and so that fate's antithesis; while what I have called "the Mask" is an *emotional* antithesis to all that comes out of their internal nature.[19]

We find ourselves in an awkward but comprehensible semantic difficulty: the "*intellectual* daily re-creation" is clearly analogous to identification, which is an *emotional* mode—it uses the intellect for emotional ends. Similarly, the mask is a substitute for a failed emotional self, invokes a daemon much like the ego ideal, and is thus in the mode that sustains repression rather than sublimation. Yeats's characterizations confuse means with ends but otherwise indicate the two modes we have traced in the poetry since Milton's companion poems.

Yeat's syntax at first leads us to think that subjectivity reconciles emotion and intellect, self and daemon. But this is not the case. The conflict persists between a desire or need for the "re-creation" that is return and an antithetical ideal that forbids such recurrence. The id's dream of satisfaction continues now in the internalized form of "thoughts" that compensate the poet for the objects that fate snatches away. Yeats believes deeply that one's fate is to be disappointed and to lose what one has loved, and when the poet is influenced by this belief to the exclusion of daemonic considerations, the result tends to be an identification that merely brings a form of renewed narcissism. In *A Vision,* for example, Yeats seems to admire Flaubert for just such a project. Flaubert had projected a story called *La Spirale* but died before it could be written.

It would have described a man whose dreams during sleep grew in magnificence as his life grew more and more unlucky, the wreck of some love affair coinciding with his marriage to a dream princess.[20]

Creating dream princesses from the wreck of life, as Shelley's Demogorgon urges man to "hope till Hope creates / From its own wreck the thing it contemplates,"[21] is of course a significant element in Yeats's mature poetry. Harold Bloom, one of Yeats's most responsible readers, believes that even such an unlikely poem as *A Prayer for My Daughter* contains a hidden compensatory dream:

Its actual subject is not the new-born Anne Butler Yeats but Maud Gonne, and the bridegroom who ends the poem in so movingly archaic a fashion is Yeats himself, making in a phantasmagoria the marriage he was denied in life, yet ironically marrying only his own soul.[22]

Yeats's "intellectual daily re-creation," which I have set in an emotional context, is thus self's response to loss and brings about an attendant solitude that precludes a dialogue with the daemonic other that in some measure is involved in that loss. The mask is a way of evading the tendency to self-involvement or self-pity that leads to only intellectual re-creation. It is, therefore, a means of invoking the power of otherness, but without the submission or self-surrender that seemed so necessary in Keats, and which is temperamentally more difficult for Yeats.

The origin of the mask appears to lie in Yeats's recollection of those Irish tales of men and women stolen by the fairies, "some spirit or inanimate object bewitched *into their likeness* remaining in their stead," and he finds in such replacements his idea of the mask:

I woke one night to find myself lying upon my back with all my limbs rigid, and to hear a ceremonial measured voice, which did not seem to be mine, speaking through my lips, "We make an image of him who sleeps," it said, "and it is not him who sleeps, and we call it Emmanuel." [23]

Yeats, rigid in sleep, becomes the "inanimate object" left by the fairies, and speaks as with their power to enchant—the ceremonial "voice" of the Enchanter now made one with the poet's voice. The mask serves the same purpose as the symbol therefore.

Is the voice of enchantment so readily assimilated? one cannot help wondering. "It is not him who sleeps": the assimilation seems to require a diminution of self, just as intellectual re-creation excludes otherness. Yeats's task, as he himself recognizes, is to strike a balance between emotion and intellect, in which self meets otherness with neither full loss nor complete assimilation. This is a process that must depend upon a retention of self as well as self-surrender, both of which are made difficult by the mask. Yeats thought of Villon and Dante as "supreme masters of tragedy"—since the moment of encounter is as close to tragedy as lyrical poetry gets—because, ironically, they acknowledged their own poverty. Those two poets, Yeats observes, "would not, when they speak through their art, change their luck; yet they are mirrored in all the suffering of desire." [24] The suffering of desire is Yeats's true *métier* and represents necessary submission as well as the wish for encounter. The mask is an instantaneous change of luck, an avoidance of self that also avoids necessary self-acceptance and the forgiveness that is one element of poetic love.

The problem of the mask turns on the dialectical relation of sorrow and joy, submission and strength and, finally, on the poet's relationships to world and otherness.

> Because there is submission in a pure sorrow, we should sorrow alone over what is greater than ourselves, nor too soon admit that greatness, but all that is less than we are should stir us to some joy, for pure joy masters and impregnates; and so to world end, strength shall laugh and wisdom mourn. [25]

Yeats's theory of the mask has as its goal the strength that masters, but the sense of a presence "greater than ourselves" that cannot be assimilated is antipodal to this and seems to require the sorrow that is submission. The mask makes possible a passionate joy that circumvents self-consciousness, then. But Yeats is also aware that "the passions, when we know that they cannot find fulfilment, become vision. . . ." [26] These are frustrated or starved passions, those that have run into a restraint that involves that "greater" power, the daemon that seems an ego ideal.

Yeats specifies his difference with Shelley and with his own early poetry by choosing passion in place of the wisdom that must mourn. The passions may become vision and, Yeats continues, "a vision, whether we wake or sleep, prolongs its power by rhythm and pattern, the wheel where the world is butterfly." As in Keats, there is a self-surrender necessary to vision, for "if we become interested in ourselves" we pass out of it.[27] And one may see the relation of submission to poetic love here, and to poetic voice. In a characteristically rich letter written to his father on March 14, 1916, Yeats says that "I express my love in rhythm." In distinguishing rhythm from the mechanical "cadence" of "music-hall verses," Yeats claims that only poetical rhythm "suggests a voice shaken with joy or sorrow." [28] These are Yeats's higher strains, those that leave behind the mask and all evasions and invoke a vision that the poet hopes is joyous or innocent. In this moment the self is forgotten or surrendered, but a form of self-possession is nevertheless achieved: now, "whether we wake or sleep," "we are taken up into a clear light and are forgetful even of our own names and actions and yet in perfect possession of ourselves murmur like Faust, 'Stay, moment,' and murmer in vain." [29]

"Do I wake or sleep?" Keats asked, and Yeats answers that the poet both wakes and sleeps as he attains self-possession. This is Yeats's great middle period, in which he attempts to give up Shelley's contemplative mode and the wisdom that comes only in the consummation of time. And if a poet could, after all, free himself from the precursor whose otherness informs his early sense of poetic identity, we should see Yeats as original now, as Crane in his brokenness thought he found "What I hold healed, original now, and pure. . . ." Bloom sees in the close of *The Wild Swans at Coole,* written in October, 1916, Yeats's attempt to break completely from Shelley's influence, represented in the departing swans. But Bloom adds that "the prophecy was not fulfilled." [30] Nor does it seem that it could be, for otherness intrudes even upon Yeats's Faustian self-possession. In one of his last letters, almost certainly read by Yeats, Shelley describes his existence on the bay of Lerici: "If the past and the future could be obliterated, the present would content me so well that I could say with Faust to the passing moment, "Remain, thou, thou art so beautiful." [31]

While consciously turning away from Shelley, Yeats nevertheless has occupied his space. What in Yeats's initial phase of development was a desire for the symbol becomes now a desire for self-possession, but one in which wholeness is complicated by the presence of otherness: the daemon is a form of Shelley's contemplative wisdom. Daemon and man may be antithetical, but to enter the daemon's arena is to court a deathly consummation as surely as invoking intellectual completion did earlier, for self-possession is mocked by the daemon's or soul's possession of *itself*:

> When all sequence comes to an end, time comes to an end, and the soul puts on the rhythmic or spiritual body or luminous body and contemplates all the events of its memory and every possible impulse in an eternal possession of itself in one single moment.[32]

A central ambiguity of Yeats's subjectivity, then, is that the daemon is a version of the soul and retains elements of the earlier intellectual idealism. The quest for self-possession, the attempt to achieve the single moment of crisis, leads to a union with the daemon, but also to the death of the senses, as had the earlier quest for the intellectual symbol. Yeats deeply wishes to humanize the daemon, the ghostly figure of the Shelleyan wisdom he seeks to reject, but it is more than less accurate to see the daemon as Yeats's true muse, which, like the ambivalent muses of Shelley and Keats, harbors a potential destructiveness as well as beneficence. Thus the various spokesmen for God and soul in Yeats's poetry offer at most a possible gathering of the poet into a possible eternity, and at least a threat to the poet's necessary ability to rise above remorse.

The mask is an attempt to evade the destructive portion of the daemon, and in his explanation of the reasons for adopting a mask, Yeats provides us also with an explanation of the nature of the daemonic threat:

> all happiness depends on the energy to assume the mask of some other life, on a re-birth as something not one's self . . . in playing a game like that of a child where one loses the infinite pain of self-realization, in a grotesque or solemn painted face put on that one may hide from the terror of judgement.[33]

This statement of a sense of judgment, which appears in *Per Amica Silentia Lunae,* comes from a diary Yeats kept in 1909. There a discussion of the poet's understanding of both judgment and justice precedes his thoughts on the mask:

> The pain others give passes away in their later kindness, but that of our own blunders, especially when they hurt our vanity, never passes away. Our own acts are isolated and one act does not buy absolution for another. They are always present before a strangely abstract judgment. . . . Looking back I find only one offence which is as painful to me as a hurt to vanity. It was done to a man who died shortly after. Because of his death, it has not been touched by the transforming hand—tolerant Nature has not rescued it from Justice.[34]

Yeats sees wisdom necessitating mourning and the daemon leading to death, and takes up the mask as a means of undoing that death and that judgment. The mask thus has as its purpose the protection of the emotional self, though it effects this by a reaction to one's own life: it reflects fear

rather than forgiveness, whereas the daemon that is a judgmental force needs to be humanized by self-acceptance if
Unity of Being is to be achieved. One of the terrors of judgment to Yeats is that Nature cannot rescue us from Justice,
or to choose an alternative vocabulary, emotion, as he fears,
cannot save us from intellect. Yeats increasingly desires joy,
passion, ecstasy, but *believes* the daemon is his destiny.

When, therefore, in a statement that is often cited, he
writes that he hopes the elaborate machinery of *A Vision* will
help him to "hold in a single thought reality and justice," he
is not suggesting, various critics to the contrary, only that he
wishes to combine the real and the ideal, but that he wants
his own reality to be consonant with "Justice." [35] That is, he
desires forgiveness. As we have seen, Yeats believes that literature is the forgiveness of sin; and sin is the self's trans-
gression of the judgment that is the ego ideal.

Yeats's categories of "reality and justice" have as their
source the "dower" of Wisdom of Shelley's Prince Athanase:
"His soul had wedded Wisdom, and her dower / Is love and
justice." Yeats *dualizes* Shelley's seemingly monistic idealism,
dividing subjective "reality" from an outer justice, perhaps
because he could not subsume self-consciousness to wisdom.
Yet Freud suggests that it is Yeats's own early idealism that is
internalized as a voice of self-criticism, a thought that at least
helps to explain the means by which the daemon, which
after all is the buried self or soul, becomes also a judgmental
agent. Freud surmises that an extreme commitment to an
object, or a sublimated commitment to an idea, may alter
radically the nature of the ego ideal or super-ego: *"The object
has been put in the place of the ego ideal."* [36]

That Yeats's early devotion allows Shelley's intellectual
idealism to become a part of the daemon of self-criticism
seems reasonably certain, and it seems clear too that Yeats's
daemon embodies a kind of absolute justice that also is characteristic of the ego ideal that is conscience. In Shelley and in
Keats, as well as in Yeats, the poet unveils the muse and
enters her realm of vision only to find the threat of death, as
if the ego even at that moment were abandoned by the

super-ego. Geoffrey Hartman, we recall, finds all romantic surmise or imaginative quest tinged by a penseroso element that darkens the visionary experience. There is a melancholy at the core of vision in Keats's odes, in Shelley's later poems, and in the later versions of the voice of the supreme Enchanter in Yeats, as though to be embraced by the muse were to suffer a kind of death—God, Yeats wrote in an early poem, burns nature with a kiss. In place of this completion, self might well choose emotion or the mask, though to choose the latter is to relinquish the hope of reconciling the antinomies of self and soul, ego and ego ideal.

In a number of Yeats's later poems the opposition between contrary truths takes the form of a dialogue (explicit or not), between an acknowledged *emotional* self and an *intellectual* daemon, in which self seeks to justify emotional existence and the desire for the spectacle of life in the face of the daemon's summons to a higher virtue that seems much like death. Keats learned in *The Fall* that the purgatorial steps must be ascended and the power of Moneta faced, though it threatens to make a ghost of the poet. Yeats tends to turn from this threat by consigning intellectual belief to the realm of the not human, the region of darkness that is now a source of terror to the poet who earlier invoked its sublimity. In *A Dialogue of Self and Soul,* Self attempts to make its reality—including its past—one with abstract justice, but Soul scorns the "thought" that is man's life and urges intellectual completion:

> Fix every wandering thought upon
> That quarter where all thought is done:
> > Who can distinguish darkness from the soul?

Soul speaks from the quarter of the supreme Enchanter and his antithetical councils, but that choice has grown bitter to Yeats, and Self sees there only death. Though Soul speaks of the possibility of deliverance from "the crime of death and birth," as Shelley in *Adonais* had fixed his thought upon the starlit air that redeems us from the "eclipsing Curse / of birth," Self needs a form of forgiveness that is more immediate. Yet it is just this forgiveness in life that the antithetical Soul cannot grant, and the great monologue of the second part of the poem, in which the power of otherness is more directly acknowledged, is motivated by its refusal:

> Only the dead can be forgiven;
> But when I think of that my tongue's a stone.

A younger Yeats thought those who spoke too much of the things of faery felt their tongues turn to stone.[37] But what is frozen in Soul's statement is the voice of intellectual enchantment. In place of this uncertain heaven, Self chooses the happiness of the body and primary existence, and so hides from the terror of judgment. Self gives up a possible purity for the ditches that are "impure," remains an "unfinished man" rather than the antithetical "whole" man, but thinks it has achieved the self-forgiveness that, in a further irony of influence, Yeats found in Shelley in 1900: "his Cythna bids the sailors be without remorse, for all that live are stained as they are. It is thus, she says, that time marks men and their thoughts for the tomb." [38] When Self does away with remorse it attains the momentarily complete but perilous contentment of the primary poet, who has rejected any passing into the region of divinity:

> forgive myself the lot!
> When such as I cast out remorse
> So great a sweetness flows into the breast
> We must laugh and we must sing,
> We are blest by everything,
> Everything we look upon is blest.

Yeats sings in his new solitude, but his isolation is from the daemon rather than the marketplace, for the daemon in the poem is the darkness that cannot forgive. Self attains the sweetness of emotional completion by avoiding Soul's intellectual summons, and, in its admitted blindness, ironically sees blessings in everything.

There is an authentic note of victory at the close of the poem, but also a narrowness of vision, a reduction of desire.

Yeats perhaps intends the irony of blind seeing, but this is
not the same blindness to outer reality that Keats feared in
the sublime, for Keats knew that so blinded one could no
longer see the spectacle of life. Self's triumph therefore
seems partial, and the reader senses a not altogether satisfying simplicity in the last three lines. When Self declares, "I
am content to live it all again," we understand that this is a
desire for return and can relate this to emotional need, but
there is more declared than won, and we may feel a consequent lack of authenticity. What the poet seems to have
relinquished is a voice of intense lyricism in which we hear
both the joy of strength and the mournfulness of wisdom,
which Yeats describes as a necessary conjunction in the late
essay *A General Introduction for My Work* (1937): "What moves
me and my hearer is a vivid speech that has no laws except
that it must not exorcise the ghostly voice. I am awake and
asleep, at my moment of revelation, self-possessed in self-
surrender." [39] Here is Yeats at his most receptive and finest,
alive to the "possibility" that is the ghost's dower, yet humanizing that voice as he possesses it.

The description of self-possession in self-surrender which,
as we have seen, seems crucial to this poetic ideal, arises I
believe from Yeats's understanding of the tragic hero as a
man at the boundary of redemption. Yeats earlier wrote that
"Shakespeare's persons, when the last darkness has gathered
about them, speak out of an ecstasy that is one-half the self-
surrender of sorrow, and one-half the last playing and
mockery of the victorious sword before the defeated
world." [40] This "ecstasy" is the true voice of feeling in the
poet, reflecting his openness to the sorrows of the "last darkness" of the sublime and his strength in remaking the world.
In his *General Introduction* Yeats recalls Lady Gregory stating
that "Tragedy must be a joy to the man who dies" if a play is
to succeed, and Yeats concludes that it is not "any different
with lyrics, songs, narrative poems. . . ." [41] An entry from
"The Death of Synge," in the *Autobiography*, finds this sorrowful ecstasy in Hamlet at the graveside: "I feel in *Hamlet*,
as so often in Shakespeare, that I am in the presence of a

soul lingering on the storm-beaten threshold of sanctity." [42] If in the context of time vision is a privileged "moment," this is its region, a trysting-place that is a threshold between worlds, the meeting place of the emotional world and an intellectual heaven, at which the man pauses and the voice is tinged with enchantment. Hamlet is self-possessed by virtue of his passion and achieves a tragic voice as he surrenders self-consciousness and fear of the sublime. The sanctity of the soul and the heaven of the complete poet lie before him—the gifts of an acknowledged sorrow and a certain joy.

I think it is this lack of a voice that acknowledges both tragedy and strength, yet is not self-conscious, that makes the close of *A Dialogue of Self and Soul* seem partial; and perhaps too this is the reason that whereas the tragic hero sees in his blindness, Self is blind in its seeing. In the conclusion of the poem the ghostly voice *is* exorcised, the poet turns away from the threshold at which he becomes knit to the daemon. We are left with a folk song, but we do not hear the voice of those supreme councils: revelation is only of the self. To cross the threshold of sanctity is to discover one's true genius, but, the poet fears, one does so only to die, and Yeats with age tends to turn from this crossing, and from its genius.

In a late letter, Yeats proceeds from a consideration of Rilke's idea of death as a completion to his own somewhat different conception. "According to Rilke a man's death is born with him and if his life is successful . . . his nature is completed by his final union with it." Though this is much like his own idea of union with the daemon, Yeats prefers to consider life a series of sensuous images, in which one "sensuous image leads to another because they are never analyzed." Death, then, is a moment of crisis: "At *The Critical Moment*" the images "are dissolved by analysis," and when "all the sensuous images are dissolved we meet true death." [43] Analysis is here much like the contemplative wisdom that Yeats earlier thought would lead Shelley's soul to the "far household" of the "undying gods," if he would but brood over the "image of his secret life." What in 1900 was

transcendence or consummation is now death, and when
Yeats in the letter states that "All men with subjective na-
tures move towards a possible ecstasy, all with objective na-
tures towards a possible wisdom," we understand that he is
separating himself from Shelley's failed wisdom by means of
the radical and unexpected implication that Shelley is an objective poet. "Wisdom," the poet declares in *Blood and the
Moon,* "is the property of the dead, / A something incompatible with life. . . ."

By directing his sympathies to the arena of natural or
primary existence, Yeats completes the poetic journey he
thought Shelley only began, though the reader recognizes
that such narrowness yields only another unresolved an-
tinomy. When we encounter a situation in which a speaker is
struck by the daemon's lightning but rejects its realm, the
poem tends to fall into a category:

> "For nothing can be sole or whole
> That has not been rent."

Despite the pun, it is hard to see the soulness of Crazy Jane's
rending, or her wholeness as Unity of Being. Yeats sings of
the body's happiness as well as its pain and ugliness, but this
again is a partial joy. One of course may admire this kind of
exclusion and this poem, but we at least need to recognize
that what seems to be Yeats's authentic and undeniably great
voice, growing out of an ecstasy that is born in both sorrow
and victory, is absent here, as it is in most of the poems that
limit themselves to emotional completion—even if this seems
to include a variety of human suffering.

> "That some stream of lightning
> From the old man in the skies
> Can burn out that suffering
> No right-taught man denies.
> But a coarse old man am I,
> I choose the second-best."
> [*The Wild Old Wicked Man*]

But when Yeats speaks with the passion that is a kind of love, he need not choose the "second-best," for he is capable of lingering at the threshold of sanctity more convincingly than most poets of our time. His problem always is to hold himself open to the suffering in ecstasy, to the daemon that both loves and destroys, and this I think he achieves in one of his certain late masterpieces, *The Man and the Echo*. The daemon here, because revelation is at least partly from the self, merely echoes the words of Man, who is all men as well as the poet. These repetitions always threaten, yet Yeats does not shrink from what he elsewhere calls the heart's discovery of itself, broken but seeking no pity, not even of God.

> In a cleft that's christened Alt
> Under broken stone I halt
> At the bottom of a pit
> That broad noon has never lit.

Here in a purgatorial arena we halt in anticipation of an encounter with otherness. Man shouts a secret "to the stone" that is the tongue of Soul or daemon when it pronounces the sentence that Man implicitly now, as Self earlier, struggles against:

> Only the dead can be forgiven;
> But when I think of that my tongue's a stone.

The "secret" is that "All that I have said and done . . . Turns into a question," which Man offers as a series of questions that seek forgiveness, leading to an overwhelming question in the last stanza. Self in the *Dialogue* had been content to follow to its source every event "in action or in thought," but Man doubts what he has "said and done."

> Did that play of mine send out
> Certain men the English shot?
> Did words of mine put too great strain
> On that woman's reeling brain?
> Could my spoken words have checked

That whereby a house lay wrecked?
And all seems evil until I
Sleepless would lie down and die.

In 1906 Yeats thought the complete poet might "come to
share in the dignity of the saint" because he "had done so
much for the word's sake," but here sanctity seems more distant as the poet grows to doubt his own past use of words.

What keeps Man from total despair is Echo's harshly selective repetition of the phrase "Lie down and die," which becomes an injunction that directs the poet to necessary death.
We do not know whether Echo is the voice of the outward
Enchanter or of internalized doubt, merely that the daemon
is destructive here, a voice much like the super-ego that
creates a deep melancholy as it threatens to abandon the
ego. From this spiritual depth the Man recovers, pledging to
go on with the "spiritual intellect's great work," for man

till his intellect grows sure
That all's arranged in one clear view,
Pursues the thoughts that I pursue,
Then stands in judgment on his soul,
And, all work done, dismisses all
Out of intellect and sight
And sinks at last into the night.

Man progresses from the despair of the opening lines to this
hope that we can be self-judging, can appropriate to the self
or ego the admonishing power of the daemonic Echo, and
possess the soul by judging it. That done, Man passes to the
dissolution of the critical moment, in which judgment is an
analysis that dismisses life's sensuous images, and Man, no
longer in hiding, crosses "at last" a dark threshold. But Echo
repeats only a part of this frail hope, turning Man again to
the desolation of reality: "Into the night."

Like Keats before Moneta in *The Fall of Hyperion,* Man
struggles valiantly to redeem that less and less human voice:

O Rocky Voice,
Shall we in that great night rejoice?

All of creation shivers in this cry of restrained ecstasy, in which Man turns from his haunted past and confronts a future that he cannot distinguish from darkness. This is Yeats in his most "intense lyricism," in Hartman's phrase, humanizing a sublimity it is death to approach, in a voice that sounds the depths of both victory over the natural world and sorrow before a greatness beyond ourselves. The entire poem moves toward this question, for only in a question can that greatness be acknowledged and faced, in words that with tragic joy express both love and need.

Man lingers for one more question—"What do we know but that we face / One another in this place"—but then withdraws from this confrontation, this muted hope for dialogue.

> But hush, for I have lost the theme,
> Its joy or night seem but a dream;
> Up there some hawk or owl has struck,
> Dropping out of sky or rock,
> A stricken rabbit is crying out,
> And its cry distracts my thought.

The movement from a possible rejoicing to this self-silencing indicates the end of surmise, but there is much said in these lines. Yeats's model is Coleridge's *Dejection* ode, which similarly moves from a hope that "We in ourselves rejoice" to a hushing of self-questioning and a turning away from surmise and the raving wind:

> But hush! there is a pause of deepest silence!
> . . . .
> It tells another tale, with sounds less deep and loud!
>   A tale of less affright,
>   And tempered with delight,
> As Otway's self had framed the tender lay,—
>   'Tis of a little child
>   Upon a lonesome wild,
> Not far from home, but she hath lost her way:
> And now moans low in bitter grief and fear,

> And now screams loud, and hopes to make
>   her mother hear.

Yeats avoids the sentimentalism that intrudes upon Coleridge's lines by sustaining a dual possibility: Man's hope is to face the daemon without the self-consciousness that would imply fear of abandonment, and so we find a purposeful uncertainty—"joy or night," "hawk or owl," "sky or rock." Man makes of Echo a voice of possible enchantment, in which joy, sky, and the hawk stand as emblems of the day against the contrary emblems of the night. Much earlier, Yeats had thought there could be nothing more important than to "cry out" that poetry, romance, and intellectual beauty were signals of the supreme Enchanter. Here the "crying out" is of mortal uncertainty, a momentary lingering before a threshold the poet cannot cross without giving up the world that only in him has grown intelligible.

From the perspective of the poet's later work, or the later work of Keats, among others, the remembrance I have chosen as an epigraph to this chapter takes on a powerful nostalgia—a reverie over childhood that does not survive the harsher contraries to come. For the poet learns that he is not an elemental god or magician, for he does not have the necessary self-possession for this; and he learns that he cannot die on the shore of immense expectations (any more than Keats could be sublimed to Apollo), for ecstasy must become a self-surrender that includes forgiveness. The later versions of these desires do not "compete" so much as they interact: knit to each other, or intersecting with each other, they transport us to that sacred ground where the almost ritualistic struggle between poet and other, subject and object, is enacted. Though his rhythm may shudder and his love falter before a greatness it is death to approach, the poet now never speaks with the voice of self—he speaks also for us, as Hamlet speaks for us, or as Imogen does, in the confrontation that must always be entered though it can never be won. Man, as Yeats writes, can embody truth but he cannot know it.

Notes

CHAPTER 1

1 Geoffrey Hartman, "Romantic Poetry and the Genius Loci," in *Beyond Formalism: Literary Essays 1958–1970* (New Haven: Yale University Press, 1970), p. 322 (hereafter cited as "Genius Loci").

2 Yeats of course intends this as allegory: the poet, as he says, never writes as to "someone at the breakfast table." William Butler Yeats, "A General Introduction for My Work," in *Essays and Introductions* (New York: Macmillan, 1961), p. 509.

3 Victor Brombert, "The Happy Prison: A Recurring Romantic Metaphor," in *Romanticism: Vistas, Instances, Continuities,* ed. David Thorburn and Geoffrey Hartman (Ithaca: Cornell University Press, 1973), p. 71.

4 "Genius Loci," p. 333.

5 Kenneth Burke, *The Philosophy of Literary Form: Studies in Symbolic Action,* rev. ed. (New York: Vintage, 1957), p. 223.

6 The essay was first published in 1945 and is reprinted in *The Liberal Imagination: Essays on Literature and Society,* by Lionel Trilling (New York: Anchor Books, 1953), pp. 155–75.

7 Burke, *Philosophy of Literary Form,* p. 223.

8 Burke, *Philosophy of Literary Form,* p. 241.

9 *Philosophy of Literary Form,* p. 243, n. 9. Burke's attempt to use communication rather than wish as the mode of analysis reflects his interest in emphasizing the sociological rather than psychological component of poetic motivation. This is a way of diminishing the subjective element, but his later view of the similarity of communication to love and libido brings us closer to the relationship of poet to other, the subject of the present study.

10 Burke, *Philosophy of Literary Form,* pp. 242–43.

11 Sigmund Freud, *On Narcissism: An Introduction,* Standard Edition of the Complete Psychological Works of Sigmund Freud (hereafter cited as Standard Edition), trans. and ed. James Strachey (London: Hogarth Press, 1957), 14:75.

12 William Butler Yeats, "Per Amica Silentia Lunae," in *Essays*

(New York: Macmillan, 1924), p. 500 (hereafter cited as "Per Amica Silentia Lunae").

13   Hartman, "Romanticism and Anti-Self-Consciousness," in *Beyond Formalism,* p. 304.

14   See Norman Maclean, "From Action to Image: Theories of the Lyric in the Eighteenth Century," in *Critics and Criticism,* ed. R. S. Crane (Chicago: University of Chicago Press, 1952), pp. 408–60.

15   Rosemund Tuve, *Images and Themes in Five Poems by Milton* (Cambridge, Mass.: Harvard University Press, 1957), p. 24.

16   Leslie Brisman, *Milton's Poetry of Choice and Its Romantic Heirs* (Ithaca: Cornell University Press, 1973), p. 12. A rich and highly important study of both the dynamics of poetic choice and the relation of Milton to the Romantics. Hereafter cited as *Milton's Poetry of Choice.*

17   The essay on Morris is a basic statement of Yeats's views on the poetry of natural abundance or primary poetry. See Yeats, "The Happiest of the Poets," in *Essays and Introductions,* pp. 53–64.

18   *Milton's Poetry of Choice,* p. 24.

19   Milton, *Paradise Lost,* I, 97.

20   Sublimation is a "way by which those demands can be met *without* involving repression" (*On Narcissism,* Standard Edition, 14:95).

21   See the Anima Hominis section of "Per Amica Silentia Lunae," especially p. 488. Freud frequently doubted the effectiveness of repression, for he had little faith in man's ability to give up any source of satisfaction. Occasionally he wondered whether a source is not renounced so much as turned to its opposite, a possibility that would accord equally well with Yeats's opposing virtue.

22   See Geoffrey Hartman, *Wordsworth's Poetry: 1787–1814* (New Haven: Yale University Press, 1964), pp. 8–12, for Hartman's initial statement of the role of surmise in Romantic poetry. The idea has proved crucial to numerous later discussions.

23   *Wordsworth's Poetry,* p. 11.

24   Keats's copy of Milton is now at the Keats House in Hampstead. The annotations have been reprinted recently in *The Romantics on Milton: Formal Essays and Critical Asides,* ed. Joseph Anthony Wittreich, Jr. (Cleveland: The Press of Case Western Reserve University, 1970), pp. 553–60.

25   "Per Amica Silentia Lunae," p. 505. I discuss this quotation in the context of Yeats's own work in chapter 5.

26   One might look first to the revised edition of Harold Bloom's *The Visionary Company: A Reading of English Romantic Poetry* (Ithaca: Cornell University Press, 1971), pp. 7–15.

27   Sigmund Freud, *Group Psychology and the Analysis of the Ego*, Standard Edition, 18:112–13.

28   *Group Psychology*, Standard Edition, 18:13; Freud's emphasis.

29   *On Narcissism*, Standard Edition, 14:100.

30   Standard Edition, 14:70.

31   Sigmund Freud, *Totem and Taboo*, Standard Edition, 13:85. Freud tends to use the word "thought" in somewhat the same way that Milton uses "surmise."

32   Freud, *Totem and Taboo*, Standard Edition, 13:88.

33   Freud, *Totem and Taboo*, Standard Edition, 13:85. Freud took the expression from a patient and used it frequently. It fits neatly with his contrary view of the omnipotence of reality.

34   *Totem and Taboo*, Standard Edition, 13:90.

35   *Totem and Taboo*, Standard Edition, 13:87.

36   Freud, *On Narcissism*, Standard Edition, 14:91.

37   See Kenneth Allott, "The Ode to Psyche," in *John Keats: A Reassessment*, ed. Kenneth Muir (Liverpool: Liverpool University Press, 1958), pp. 74–94.

38   *Totem and Taboo*, Standard Edition, 13:90.

39   Sigmund Freud, *An Autobiographical Study*, 20:72.

40   Geoffrey Hartman, "I. A. Richards and the Dream of Communication," in *The Fate of Reading and Other Essays* (Chicago: University of Chicago Press, 1975), p. 33.

41   "Poetry and Tradition," in *Essays and Introductions*, p. 255.

CHAPTER 2

1   Reprinted in *The Romantics Reviewed: Contemporary Reviews of British Romantic Writers*, ed. Donald H. Reiman (New York: Garland, 1972), part C, I, p. 429.

2   Thus, for example, Yeats contrasts himself as poet—the "fleeting thing that held out its hand" ("Discoveries," in *Essays and Introductions*, p. 271)—with the saint: "The saint alone is not deceived, neither thrusting with his shoulder nor holding out unsatisfied hands" ("Per Amica Silentia Lunae," in *Essays*, p. 500).

3   The section on mythmaking, of which this passage is a part,

had a formative influence on Keats: reflections of it can be seen in a number of the early poems and in *Hyperion*. Compare, for instance, the herdsman's imagining a "beardless Youth" creating the "distant strain" he hears (IV, 851–60), with Clymene's perception of Apollo and his music (*Hyperion*, II, 272–95).

4   Sigmund Freud, *The Ego and the Id,* Standard Edition, 19:58.

5   "False Themes and Gentle Minds," in *Beyond Formalism*, p. 288.

6   Walter Jackson Bate, *John Keats* (New York: Oxford University Press, 1966), p. 125.

7   *The Letters of John Keats: 1814–1821,* ed. Hyder Edward Rollins (Cambridge, Mass., 1958), 1:405 (hereafter cited as *Letters*).

8   Bate, *John Keats,* p. 128.

9   *The Autobiography of William Butler Yeats* (New York: Collier Books, 1965), p. 170.

10   M. A. Goldberg, *The Poetics of Romanticism: Toward a Reading of John Keats* (Ohio: Antioch Press, 1969), p. 77.

11   Glen O. Allen, "The Fall of Endymion: A Study in Keats's Intellectual Growth," *Keats-Shelley Journal* 6 (1957): 37–57. In his *Keats the Poet* (Princeton: Princeton University Press, 1973), Stuart M. Sperry notes the influence of Allen's reading of the poem on his own approach.

12   In *The Romantic Sublime* (Baltimore: Johns Hopkins Press, 1976).

13   *The Complete Works of Percy Bysshe Shelley,* ed. R. Ingpen and W. E. Peck (New York: Charles Scribner's Sons, 1965), 6:202.

14   "The Symbolism of Poetry," in *Essays and Introductions*, p. 159.

15   Paul de Man's penetrating essay "Literary History and Literary Modernity" is included in his recent *Blindness and Insight: Essays in the Rhetoric of Contemporary Criticism* (New York: Oxford University Press, 1971), p. 148.

16   "Per Amica Silentia Lunae," in *Essays,* p. 505.

17   "Discoveries," in *Essays and Introductions*, p. 277.

18   "Poetry and Tradition," in *Essays and Introductions*, pp. 252–53.

19   *The 'Uncanny,'* Standard Edition, 17:235.

20   In this context, it is interesting that Endymion thinks of the moon as his sister (III, 145). She is Apollo's sister, in fact.

CHAPTER 3

1   *Letters,* 1:185. This is also the letter in which Keats tells Bailey of a favorite "Speculation," that "we shall enjoy ourselves here after by having what we called happiness on Earth repeated in

a finer tone and so repeated. . . ." Keats suggests that such a fate "can only befall those who delight in sensation," thus implying a connection between the mode of repetition and sensation or the simple imagination. These are what I have termed "emotional" imaginings, making possible the solacing thought of retention, and picturing heaven as an improvement of sense ("the Prototype must be here after," Keats writes). Perhaps, considering Freud's ambiguity about the efficacy of repression, this single bright surmise underlies both emotional and repressive modes, where the latter is merely the antithesis or "opposing virtue" of the former.

2 "Prometheus Unbound," in *Essays and Introductions,* p. 425.
3 *The Keats Circle: Letters and Papers and More Letters and Poems of the Keats Circle,* ed. Hyder Edward Rollins, 2d ed. (Cambridge, Mass.: Harvard University Press, 1965), 1:25.
4 Harold Bloom's comment appears in *Yeats* (New York: Oxford University Press, 1970), pp. 18, 92; for Allen see "The Fall of Endymion"; see Stuart Sperry's "The Allegory of *Endymion,*" *Studies in Romanticism* 2 (1962): 38–53.
5 The annotations were first collected by the Rev. J. Freeman Clarke and later reprinted by H. Buxton Forman in his edition of Keats. As noted above, they have been published more recently in Wittreich's *The Romantics on Milton.*
6 *The Romantics on Milton,* p. 553.
7 Charles Cowden Clarke and Mary Cowden Clarke, *Recollections of Writers* (New York: Charles Scribner's Sons, 1878, pp. 125–26.
8 *The Keats Circle,* 2:274.
9 *Letters,* 1:281.
10 *The Romantics on Milton,* pp. 554, 557.
11 *The Romantics on Milton,* p. 557; my emphasis of Keats's comments.
12 *The Romantics on Milton,* p. 557.
13 *The Romantics on Milton,* p. 559.
14 *The Romantics on Milton,* p. 559.
15 *The Keats Circle,* 2:275–76.
16 *Recollections of Writers,* p. 126.
17 This point is persuasively argued by Geoffrey Hartman in "Milton's Counterplot," in *Milton: Modern Essays in Criticism,* ed. Arthur Barker (New York: Oxford University Press, 1965), pp. 386–97. The essay has been reprinted in *Beyond Formalism,* pp. 42–57.

18   Neil H. Hertz, "Wordsworth and the Tears of Adam," *Studies in Romanticism* 7 (1967): 15–33.

19   Hartman, "Milton's Counterplot," pp. 390–96.

20   *Letters,* 1:274.

21   My emphasis of Hazlitt's comments. As well as being the probable source of Keats's "sublime pathetic," Hazlitt may have provided Keats with his understanding of both sublimity and pathos, though of course the terms were widely used. In his edition of *Select Poets of Great Britain* (London, 1825), Hazlitt uses the two terms as evaluative categories for past poets. Thus, "Gray's sublimity was borrowed and mechanical," whereas Milton "has sublimity in the highest degree" and "pathos in a degree next to the highest" (pp. xiv, x). The volume was too late for Keats to have used but illustrates Hazlitt's use of the terms.

22   My emphasis. The *Defence* is usefully reprinted in *Shelley's Prose: or the Trumpet of a Prophecy,* ed. David Lee Clark (Albuquerque: University of New Mexico Press, 1954); see p. 295 for the quoted material.

23   Morris Dickstein, *Keats and His Poetry: A Study in Development* (Chicago: University of Chicago Press, 1971), p. 129. The book is especially valuable for its discussion of the early poems, which are essential to any consideration of Keats's poetic development.

24   Sperry, *Keats the Poet,* p. 182.

25   *Letters,* 1:387.

26   *Letters,* 2:102.

27   Bate, *John Keats,* pp. 604–05n.

28   Geoffrey Hartman, "Spectral Symbolism and the Authorial Self: An Approach to Keats's *Hyperion,*" *Essays in Criticism* 24, no. 1 (January, 1974), p. 5.

CHAPTER   4

1   In *Beyond Formalism,* p. 304.

2   Harold Bloom, *The Anxiety of Influence: A Theory of Poetry* (New York: Oxford University Press, 1973), p. 61.

3   "Per Amica Silentia Lunae," in *Essays,* p. 499.

4   Bate, *John Keats,* p. 487.

5   Pointed out by Harold Bloom in *A Map of Misreading* (New York: Oxford University Press, 1975), p. 153.

6   Keats, *Letters*, 1:387.
7   *The Ego and the Id*, Standard Edition, 19:29, 30.
8   Freud, *Mourning and Melancholia*, Standard Edition, 14:249.
9   *The Ego and the Id*, Standard Edition, 9:30.
10 *Group Psychology*, Standard Edition, 18:105; my emphasis.
11 Keats, *Letters*, 2:102.
12 See Geoffrey Hartman's fine essay "Poem and Ideology: A Study of Keats's 'To Autumn,' " in *Literary Theory and Structure: Essays in Honor of William K. Wimsatt*, ed. Frank Brady, John Palmer, and Martin Price (New Haven: Yale University Press, 1973), p. 324.
13 "Poem and Ideology," p. 323.
14 "Poem and Ideology," p. 313.
15 Quoted in Bate, *John Keats*, p. 244.
16 My transcription from the copy of the play at the Keats House in Hampstead.
17 "A General Introduction for My Work," in *Essays and Introductions*, p. 521.

CHAPTER 5

1   Yeats, "Symbolism in Painting," in *Essays and Introductions*, p. 146.
2   Yeats, "Magic," in *Essays and Introductions*, p. 52.
3   Yeats, "The Symbolism of Poetry," in *Essays and Introductions*, p. 161.
4   Yeats, "The Symbolism of Poetry," p. 162.
5   "The Happiest of the Poets," *Essays and Introductions*, p. 61. Though Yeats is characteristically offhanded here, the bitterness he mentions seems similar to the hatred that he finds prevalent in his own life and in others, except at those times when he is where the daemon is. In a parallel thought, though with a different vocabulary, Freud thought that ambivalence— the simultaneous love and hatred for the same object—began with the effort to overcome the Oedipal complex. Bitterness and ambivalence figure crucially in Romantic poems that treat a return to place, since a dislocating fall has usually occurred in the intervening time.
6   "At Stratford-on-Avon," in *Essays and Introductions*, pp. 106–07.
7   "Modern Poetry: A Broadcast," in *Essays and Introductions*, pp. 491–92.
8   "Per Amica Silentia Lunae," in *Essays*, p. 500.

9   *Group Psychology and the Analysis of the Ego,* Standard Edition, 18:113.

10 "The Philosophy of Shelley's Poetry," in *Essays and Introductions,* p. 95. Yeats is widely concerned with voices that come to the poet's ear, as in his image of the contemplative poet who hears "well-instructed voices" (See "Discoveries," in *Essays and Introductions,* p. 291).

11 "The Philosophy of Shelley's Poetry," in *Essays and Introductions,* p. 80; my emphasis.

12 Yeats, *Essays and Introductions,* p. 88.

13 *Essays and Introductions,* p. 271.

14 *Essays and Introductions,* p. 293; my emphasis.

15 *Essays and Introductions,* p. 66; my emphasis.

16 Yeats, *Essays and Introductions,* p. 294.

17 *Essays and Introductions,* p. 297.

18 *Essays and Introductions,* p. 71.

19 Yeats, "Four Years: 1887–1891," in *Autobiography,* p. 129.

20 Yeats, *A Vision* (New York: Macmillan, 1938), p. 70.

21 *Prometheus Unbound,* IV, 573–74.

22 *Yeats,* p. 326.

23 *Autobiography,* p. 252. Yeats was fond of this representation of the origin of the mask and the descent of the daemonic voice, and repeats it in "Per Amica Silentia Lunae," pp. 534–35.

24 *Autobiography,* p. 183.

25 Yeats, "Poetry and Tradition," in *Essays and Introductions,* pp. 252–53.

26 "Per Amica Silentia Lunae," in *Essays,* p. 505.

27 Yeats, *Essays,* p. 505.

28 *The Letters of W. B. Yeats,* ed. Allan Wade (London: Rupert Hart-Davis, 1954), pp. 608, 609.

29 Yeats, *Essays,* p. 505.

30 *Yeats,* p. 193.

31 This poignant dream of suspension comes within a month of Shelley's death and is included in a letter to John Gisborne, written on June 18, 1822.

32 Yeats, "Per Amica Silentia Lunae," in *Essays,* p. 524.

33 *Essays,* pp. 496–497.

34 *Autobiography,* p. 340.

35 George Bornstein, in *Yeats and Shelley* (Chicago: University of Chicago Press, 1970), represents the contrary view. The eighth chapter of his book takes the statement from *A Vision* as the

basis of Yeats's metaphysical system. Bornstein then identifies "reality and justice" as "evil and good" (p. 202).
36 "Group Psychology," Standard Edition, 18:213; Freud's emphasis.
37 He expresses this in "Magic," in *Essays and Introductions*, p. 51.
38 Yeats, *Essays and Introductions*, pp. 70–71.
39 *Essays and Introductions*, p. 524.
40 "Poetry and Tradition," in *Essays and Introductions*, p. 254.
41 *Essays and Introductions*, p. 523.
42 *Autobiography*, p. 354.
43 *Letters*, p. 917; Yeats's emphasis.

Index